Organ and Tissue Transplants

Organ and Tissue Transplants

Medical Miracles and Challenges

Marilyn McClellan

Enslow Publishers, Inc.

40 Industrial Road
Box 398
Berkeley Heights, NJ 07922
USA

PO Box 38
Aldershot
Hants GU12 6BP
UK

http://www.enslow.com

Library of Congress Cataloging-in-Publication Data

McClellan, Marilyn J.
   Organ and tissue transplants : medical miracles and challenges /
Marilyn McClellan.
      p. cm. — (Issues in focus)
   Summary: Explores the history of organ transplantation, as well as
its medical, ethical, financial, and personal aspects, providing
insights into the latter through stories of organ donors and recipients.
   Includes bibliographical references and index.
   ISBN-10: 0-7660-1943-8
   1. Transplantation of organs, tissues, etc.—Juvenile literature.
2. Artificial organs—Juvenile literature. [1. Transplantation of
organs, tissues, etc. 2. Artificial organs.] I. Title. II. Series: Issues
in focus (Hillside, N.J.)
RD120.76 .M38 2003
617.9'5—dc21   2002008401

ISBN-13: 978-0-7660-1943-0

Printed in the United States of America

10 9 8 7 6 5

To Our Readers:
We have done our best to make sure all Internet addresses in this book
were active and appropriate when we went to press. However, the author
and the publisher have no control over and assume no liability for the
material available on those Internet sites or on other Web sites they may
link to. Any comments or suggestions can be sent by e-mail to com-
ments@enslow.com or to the address on the back cover.

Illustration Credits: ABIOMED, Inc., p. 87; ARS Photo Unit,
U.S. Department of Agriculture, pp. 85, 91; ArtToday, pp. 34,
76; Julie Brady, p. 108; courtesy of Brigham and Women's
Hospital, pp. 25, 30; courtesy of Burton Snowboards, pp. 48,
100; Corel Corp., p. 67; courtesy of the Kidney Foundation of
Canada, p. 64; Landesmuseum, p. 20; LifeCenter Northwest,
pp. 16, 80; Marilyn McClellan, pp. 41, 44, 53; © The Nobel
Foundation, p. 59; Philip Schofield, p. 10.

Cover Illustration: Klaus Guldbrandsen, SPL, Photo
Researchers, Inc.

Contents

1

Russell's Story

High school junior Russell Schofield loved to skateboard and snowboard. He also enjoyed playing the guitar and fast-paced video games. His special gift, however, was his sense of humor. Russell loved making people laugh. He and his parents, Susan and Philip Schofield, lived in a lovely home across from his former middle school in Bellingham, Washington. His older sister, Eiron, lived ninety miles away in Seattle.

On Friday evening, March 26, 1999, Russell went out with friends. About 10:00 P.M., he and three other Sehome

High School juniors drove away from a party in his 1995 Blazer. A few minutes later they crashed when the vehicle ran off the road. The Blazer rolled several times and hit a stump on a curve of North Shore Drive.[1] Two boys were found dead at the scene. Russell and a second boy, who later recovered, were taken to St. Joseph's hospital. Russell had a ruptured esophagus and brain trauma.

At midnight, his parents heard a knock. They thought Russ was returning from the party. A Washington State trooper was at the door. He told them about the accident. It was a parent's worst nightmare. They drove to the hospital after deciding to wait until morning to call his sister. They did not want her to drive in the middle of the night while she was worried about her brother.

The Hospital

At the hospital, a Catholic nun was waiting to meet them. She reported the terrible details of the crash. Russ was just coming out of surgery. He was in critical condition. They spoke to the doctor. He told Russ's parents that his chances were slim. Eiron arrived the next morning. Family and friends came from near and far. For two days, adults and teens kept a constant vigil by his bedside. People felt a need to be present. The hospital allowed his friends to sleep in empty rooms. In the late afternoon, on March 28, the doctor gave them the news that they already knew in their hearts. Russell was not going to make it.

One by one his friends came into the intensive care room to say good-bye. They held his hand and kissed him. They cried, they laughed, and they told jokes. Most of all, they told Russ they loved him and would never forget him. It went on for hours. High school friends shared their grief and pain with the family and with each other. It was difficult for them to accept that life could end so quickly for one so young.

Russell was pronounced "brain dead" by his doctors. Medical tests confirmed that all functions of his brain had stopped. A ventilator continued to keep his organs functioning by artificially supplying oxygen to his lungs. Once the doctors removed the ventilator, Russell's body functions would shut down and his heart would stop. In the midst of their pain and grief, the Schofields learned that Russell was a perfect candidate to be an organ donor.

The hospital was required by law to report Russell's death to LifeCenter Northwest. It is the organ procurement organization (OPO) that covers the western states of Washington, Alaska, Montana, and northern Idaho. LifeCenter Northwest is one of fifty-nine OPOs in a national network. It had the responsibility to send trained experts to speak to the Schofield family about donating Russell's organs. OPOs help grieving families make informed decisions about donating their loved one's organs and tissues. They also give families the option to decline.

Russell's parents were still in shock. Two days earlier, their son had been healthy and active. Now, he was lying on a hospital bed. While his body functions

Russell Schofield, a high school junior, died after a car accident. His transplanted organs—lungs, liver, and kidneys—saved the lives of several people.

were sustained by a machine, they were being asked to consider giving away his organs. Susan Schofield said, "It was an extremely difficult moment. We learned that Russell wouldn't live, and we were asked about the possibility of organ donation. Although it seemed like a natural thing to do, we did not fully understand what it would entail."[2]

Saving Lives

One of the medical miracles of the second half of the twentieth century is the success of organ transplant operations. As these operations have more success, there is a greater shortage of needed organs. On July 19, 2002, the national patient waiting list for organ transplants had 80,312 registrations.[3] Some patients are registered at more than one transplant center. Some patients are waiting for more than one organ. But it is clear that over 75,000 Americans are waiting for organ transplants to save their lives. In contrast, there are few donors available. Thirty thousand persons each year are placed on a waiting list to receive an organ transplant. The list grows at the rate of one person every eighteen minutes.[4] The United States government continues to pass laws so that organ procurement agencies will do a better job of working with families to make more organs available to save lives.

There are two kinds of donors: live donors and cadaver donors. Live donors are persons who are living. Cadaver donors are people who have died. Live donors are often related to the patient who is dying from organ failure. They are able to share one kidney or part of their liver and still live healthy lives. Cadaver organs are taken from a body very soon after death with written permission from the donor's family. People can indicate their desire to donate their organs when they die by putting their wishes on their driver's license or in a will. Organs are fragile and begin to deteriorate at the moment of death. Russell was a perfect candidate for donation. His vital organs could be maintained on mechanical support until they could be removed.

Russell's parents never dreamed they would ever make such a difficult decision. They never thought to ask Russell his opinion on the matter. They had to decide themselves whether to donate his organs. And they wanted to include his older sister in the decision. The family decided to say yes. His parents signed all the legal documents. They put into motion a series of events that spread far beyond the city limits of Bellingham, Washington. These events changed the lives of several people.

Working Against Time

Their decision caused the transplant coordinator from LifeCenter Northwest to go into action. Russell's organs and blood were tested and matched with people listed on the national computer registry who were waiting for organs. Within hours of receiving written permission, a team of surgeons arrived at St. Joseph's hospital to recover Russell's organs. There was little time to spare. Critically ill patients

were chosen from the database of the United
Network for Organ Sharing, or UNOS. This is a computer system that lists all potential recipients based
on their blood type, body size, medical urgency, and
length of time on the waiting list. All these patients
were living with failing organs. They would die
unless a transplant was available. For a variety of
reasons, it is not unusual for patients to die while on
the waiting list for an organ. In the first place, only
the sickest people are listed for transplant. During
the past four years, over 23,000 people on the list
died waiting for an organ transplant. There are not
enough available organs to fill the need. Some people
will not find a suitable matching donor. Others will
die before an organ becomes available.

The people who received Russell's heart, liver,
and lungs needed to be matched with his blood type
and body size. Those who received the kidneys and
pancreas would also have to match his genetic tissue
type.[5] While the surgical teams worked in
Bellingham, potential recipients were contacted.
They went immediately to the hospital to prepare to
receive their new healthy organs. Many people waiting for transplants carry beepers or cell phones so
they can be informed any time of day or night when
an organ becomes available.

Critical Procedures

In Bellingham, surgeons followed a careful order
when they removed the organs from Russell's body.
The first organs they removed were the heart and

lungs. Unfortunately, the surgeon found that Russell's heart had been bruised during the accident. He informed the family that it could not be donated. He took out the heart valves for use in another patient. If Russell had lived, his heart might have healed in its natural state. It would not survive the trauma of a transplant.

Somewhere, in another hospital, a dying patient was getting ready to receive Russell's heart. The operation would be canceled at the last minute. This is the nature of transplantation. Timing is critical. At the time the organs are removed from a donor, recipients are already being prepared for surgery to receive them. People understand there is always a possibility of cancellation. But it is devastating news. The person who has been waiting knows that time might run out. He or she might die before another possible match is found.

Organs have a limited time to be transplanted after they are removed from the donor's body. To extend their life, they are immediately and gently cooled at a temperature just above freezing. They are placed in a sterile container so they may be moved safely from one location to another. Organs are placed on a bed of shaved ice in a small, portable picnic cooler. The time that organs remain usable before they are transplanted is called *ischemic* time. It is the time that the organs can survive apart from their critical blood supply. The surgeons removed Russell's lungs and rushed them by air to Colorado. They had just four to six hours to be transplanted. Two different women received them. Both were grandmothers.

Next, surgeons had from twelve to twenty-four hours
to rush the liver to a Washington hospital and transplant it into a forty-three-year-old construction
worker. They removed Russell's pancreas and
donated it for research involving the islet cells, which
produce insulin needed to convert sugar, starch, and
other food into energy. Finally, they had forty-eight to
seventy-two hours to transplant his kidneys. These
also went to two people. The first was a thirty-three-
year-old Washington man who had been waiting a
year for a needed transplant. The other was flown to
Michigan to a fifty-two-year-old man.[6]

Out of Death Comes Life

The story of Russell Schofield is tragic. His parents
were grateful that they were able to share their grief
with his friends and family and prepare for Russell's
death. But their lives were changed forever by their
loss. Russell's friends still visit often. They have
planted a memorial garden. They helped with the
first Russ Schofield Classic Skateboard Contest.
The family has received letters of appreciation thank-
ing them for their generosity and gifts from the lucky
people who are living with Russell's organs. These
are passed through the donor network. The names of
organ donors are not revealed to those who receive
the organs without permission from the donor's
family.

A year after Russell's death, the Schofields went
to the U.S. Transplant Games in Orlando, Florida. They
took part in a moving donor recognition ceremony.

These biannual Olympics-style games are a sporting competition for the recipients of transplants. They bring together donors and recipients to celebrate the precious gift of life.

Russell's mother says, "The act of compassion at a moment of devastating loss has evolved into the realization that lives were saved. No one wants to be in the position of having to decide about organ donation. Looking back, I can say it was a positive opportunity. It enabled us to move through our grief in ways we never anticipated."[7]

Questions Remain

Russell Schofield's story is one example of the dramatic advances in medicine and science over the past

The Transplant Games, held every two years, are an Olympics-style sporting event that brings together donor families and recipients.

fifty years. We live in a time where new possibilities arise for people who used to have little chance of surviving. Advances in medicine have given us new ways to heal the human body. We continue to learn more about the immune system. New surgical and diagnostic procedures are being developed. Amazing drugs are being designed in laboratories. Technology advances in the field of artificial organs. The incredible field of genetics with its discovery of cloning makes the imagination soar with medical possibilities.

However, these medical milestones also raise questions of ethics or moral principles, which need to be addressed. How do we decide who gets a transplant when more people need organs than there are organ donors? Are we changing the nature of death? Is it ethical to clone human body parts? Is it safe to use humans in experiments with artificial organs? What does religion say about these issues? None of these questions has a simple answer. Most of the answers lead to new questions. There is no doubt about it. This is an exciting, complex, and newsbreaking topic to explore.

A History

Since the beginning of time, there have been tales about body parts taken from one person or animal and put into another. The Bible says that the first man, Adam, donated his rib to make another human being. This kept Adam from being lonely in the new world. Greek mythology tells stories of physically complex beasts. The Chimera has a lion's head, a goat's body, and a dragon's tail. The Gorgons have heads of writhing snakes and tusks like a boar. A three-headed dog named Cerberus guards the entrance to the underworld.

In the sixteenth century, a variety of different artists painted a famous legend. The paintings show a pair of physicians named Saint Cosmas and Saint Damien. They are transplanting a leg from a black Moor onto their white patient after amputating his diseased limb. Angels are shown gathered at the foot of the bed. People at that time believed that patients needed divine intervention to help them to recover from surgery. These early accounts had little in common with scientific fact.

There have been extraordinary technical advancements in the field of medicine in the last century. It is now possible to replace a failing human organ with a healthy organ from another person's body. The history of organ transplantation is like a runaway train on a long slope. Advancements in the field have gathered momentum at increasing speeds. Medicine has smashed into the twenty-first century, breaking medical barriers on new and exciting frontiers. It is almost impossible today to pick up a newspaper without finding an article related to organ transplants. This subject had its roots in the early 1900s.

The First Steps

In 1906, a French doctor, Alexis Carrel, took the first giant step toward the future of organ transplantation. He was the first person to surgically join two blood vessels together. His technique was called *anastomosis*. Dr. Carrel used three sutures to shape the walls of the blood vessels. He then stitched those vessel walls together edge to edge with fine silk thread.

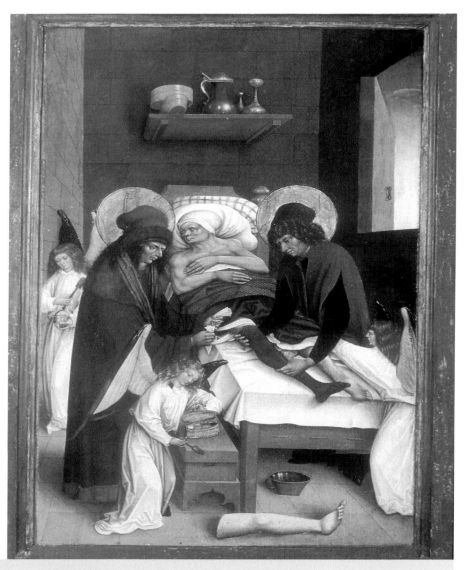

This sixteenth-century painting depicts the legend of two doctors who transplanted a leg. Formerly a panel from an altarpiece, the painting now hangs in a museum in Stuttgart, Germany.

In 1912, Dr. Carrel won the esteemed Nobel Prize in Physiology or Medicine for his work. In his Nobel acceptance lecture, he told his audience that the idea of replacing diseased organs by sound ones was not original. Many surgeons had tried it. But those surgeons had no means to resume the normal circulation through the transplanted structures.

Dr. Carrel also admitted that he could not see the future implications of his discovery. At the closing of his Nobel lecture, he said that he only solved the problem from a surgical point of view. He told his audience:

> It will only be through a . . . study of the biological relationships existing between living tissues that the problems involved will come to be solved and thereby render possible the benefits to humanity which we hope to see accomplished in the future.[1]

Dr. Carrel, a pioneer in modern surgery at the beginning of the century, predicted the problem that was to haunt transplant surgeons for one hundred years. That problem was the key to the mysteries of the human immune system.

During the first half of the twentieth century, physicians placed animal parts into human beings in attempts to transplant organs. In 1936, a Russian surgeon, Dr. U. Voronoy, reportedly performed the first human-to-human kidney transplant.[2] The kidney came from a cadaver, the body of a person who had died. Unfortunately, the patient survived with the new kidney for only two days.

Medical Discoveries During World War II

In the 1940s, Dr. Peter Medawar produced the century's most important breakthrough in the field of transplantation. He identified and described the human immune system. Dr. Medawar was a British citizen. His government approached him during World War II. They asked him to find a way to graft (or replace) skin in order to help the soldiers and civilians who had been seriously burned in bombing raids. He found that skin surgically transplanted from one part of a body to another part of the same body—called an *autograft*—would heal if the operation itself was successful. However, skin transplanted from one person to another person—called an *allograft*—shriveled up and died over time. These observations led him to describe the human immune system.

Dr. Medawar decided that the body had the ability to distinguish between friend and foe. It could recognize and kill invading viruses and bacteria. The body treats any foreign tissue as a dangerous invader. It attempts to destroy the invader in an action called *rejection*. This same immune system guards against disease. It permits the body to heal itself in times of crisis. Dr. Medawar came to a conclusion: In order to have a successful transplant, he would have to trick the human body into accepting transplanted tissue by keeping the immune system from attacking it.[3]

Another important invention during World War II was the first artificial kidney machine. This device was designed to treat kidney failure in severely injured people. It was invented by Willem Kolff, a Dutch medical researcher. It removed impurities from the blood. The machine could sustain the victims during a few weeks of temporary kidney failure until their own organs started to function again. This artificial kidney, or dialysis machine, has been perfected over the years through a series of improvements. Today over 200,000 people in the United States suffering from end-stage kidney disease are being kept alive by the newest model of this machine.[4]

The First Successful Transplant

During the beginning of the twentieth century, the focus was on the kidney. Surgically it was relatively easy to transplant. It was difficult for physicians to see otherwise young and healthy patients die because of failing kidneys. Trials of kidney transplants on both animals and humans had been unsuccessful. It was advances such as Carrel's suturing technique, Kolff's artificial kidney machine, and Medawar's understanding of the immune system that allowed programs for organ transplants to begin at a few hospitals.

The first successful kidney transplantation was a landmark case. Ronald Herrick wished to donate one of his two healthy kidneys to his identical twin, Richard, who was dying of a kidney disease. Physicians had to determine whether it was ethical to allow a well person to donate an organ. It was the first time in medical history that a healthy person was to undergo major surgery, not for his own benefit, but for the medical benefit of another.[5]

Before the operation, Richard was placed on Dr. John Merrill's adaptation of the artificial kidney machine to keep him alive. The doctor grafted skin from one brother to another. The grafts were successful because the skin was not rejected. It was decided that the men were genetically identical. It was therefore safe to transplant the kidney. The operation was performed on December 23, 1954, at the Peter Bent Brigham Hospital in Boston, Massachusetts. Dr. Joseph Murray and his surgical team removed Ronald's kidney and transplanted it into Richard.[6] Because the twins had exactly the same genetic makeup, Richard's immune system decided that the new kidney was familiar and friendly material. Richard's body accepted the new kidney as if it were his own. Richard Herrick lived for many years with his new transplant. His brother Ronald became the first successful living donor. Dr. Murray won the Nobel Prize in 1990 for this historical event and his lifetime work.

The Immune System

The medical community now understood that the immune system was responsible for the rejection of foreign tissue. They turned to finding ways to keep that system from attacking transplanted organs. By using identical twins, physicians had simply bypassed the problems of organ rejection. If they

Richard Herrick, shown here with his twin, Ronald, received his brother's kidney in 1954 in the first successful kidney transplant. He lived many years with the new kidney.

wished to continue with any success, they needed to find ways to address those problems.

Four years after the Herrick transplant, Dr. Murray transplanted another kidney. This time he used a form of radiation on the person's whole body.[7] This was to keep the immune system from attacking the new organ. A group of people working closely with Dr. Medawar believed it might be possible to give steroids to transplant patients. Steroids were shown to be effective in weakening the immune system of animals. They were found to delay the rejection of skin grafts. In Paris, Dr. Jean Hamburger was familiar with the use of steroids. He also decided that matching tissues between the organ donor and the recipient of the new organ might ease the problems of rejection.[8]

Initially, these ideas alone made little difference in the acceptance of an organ transplant. Immune specialists kept trying to understand the "biological forces" that kept transplants from being successful. A Frenchman, Jean Dausset, shed light on the specifics of the immune system. His understanding of genetics and blood cells led to a Nobel Prize in 1980. He described the first tissue group system, called the *human leukocyte antigens*. Antigens are identifying molecules that reside on the surface of cells. They are like the fingerprints of immunity. They are responsible for recognizing a threat to the immune system. They set in motion the antibodies that attack and destroy foreign tissue.[9]

Drug "Cocktails"

In 1963, the National Academy of Sciences held a conference of the world's transplant surgeons and immunologists. Two hundred forty-four organ transplants had been reported worldwide. Most had failed. Only nine patients had survived for more than one year. Participants asked the question "Is it ethical to continue?"[10] However, Dr. Thomas E. Starzl, of Denver, Colorado, reported that he was having some success with a drug "cocktail"—a mixture of different drugs. He had combined azathioprine (Imuran) and the steroid prednisone. These substances worked together to restrain the killer cells that attack foreign objects in the body. This "cocktail" approach was to be used in the future with different combinations of drugs.

Drug therapy to keep the immune system from attacking transplanted organs led to new challenges. One problem was that drugs suppressed the entire immune system. When killer cells are kept from attacking foreign substances, they are also unavailable to protect the body from disease and infection. Patients who acquired a healthy, life-prolonging organ became vulnerable to life-threatening illnesses. Furthermore, people needing a transplant already have a weak immune system because of the disease that is killing the organ. Suppressing the immune system even further can be dangerous. Another problem was that the drugs often caused serious side effects. Steroids can cause swelling, weight gain, muscle weakness, and congestive heart failure, among other problems. The possible side effects of Imuran include nausea, vomiting, and diarrhea as well as fevers, chills, and skin rash.[11]

Transplanting New Organs

Success rates in kidney transplantation relied on two factors. The first was the successful use of drug combinations. The second was the ability to match tissues between the organ donor and the recipient. Encouraged by that success, doctors looked toward transplanting other organs. Another dramatic invention opened the way for heart transplantation. In 1953, Dr. John H. Gibbon, Jr., of Philadelphia introduced the first clinically successful heart-lung machine. It was used to save the life of an eighteen-year-old girl while he repaired a hole in her heart. It is now commonplace for surgeons to stop the heartbeat for as long as several hours. During that time, circulation is maintained by modern heart-lung support equipment.

On March 1, 1963, Dr. Starzl took the liver from a three-year-old boy who had died during brain surgery. He transplanted it into another three-year-old boy who was dying of liver disease. Unfortunately, the child bled to death before the procedure was completed. That same year, Dr. James D. Hardy transplanted a lung in Mississippi. The patient survived just a few days. In 1967, Dr. Starzl performed the first successful liver transplant, at the University of Colorado by using his drug "cocktail" to control rejection. The patient lived for fourteen months.

In l967, Dr. Christiaan Barnard of Cape Town, South Africa, stunned the world by taking the heart of a young woman who had died in an automobile accident and transplanting it into Louis Washkansky. Fifty-five-year-old Washkansky was dying of diabetes and incurable heart disease. Washkansky lived only eighteen days. His surgeon gained international fame. Barnard's second heart transplant patient survived seventeen months. Dr. Norman E. Shumway performed the first United States heart transplant at Stanford University in 1968. Shumway assisted his colleague, Dr. Bruce Reitz, in the first successful double organ transplant. The patient, Mary Gohlke, received both a heart and a lung transplant on March 9, 1981. She survived for five years.

Cyclosporine

Survival rates climbed sharply following the next breakthrough. In 1970, employees of Sandoz Pharmaceuticals, a Swiss drug company, obtained soil samples while on vacation in Norway. Back in Switzerland, they extracted an antibiotic-like substance from a fungus present in the soil. This substance was named cyclosporine. A few years later, Swiss immunologist Dr. Jean-Francois Borel demonstrated to the medical community that the drug had the ability to suppress the immune system in new ways. Cyclosporine was more focused than previous drugs. It did not target all aspects of the body's immune defenses.[12] Instead, the drug blocked the production of a type of white blood cells called

T-helper cells that identify and attack transplanted tissue. Unfortunately, high doses of the drug induced the growth of cancerous tumors and were poisonous to kidneys. Doctors needed to find ways to use the smallest dosage that would both suppress the immune system without causing devastating side effects. With the use of cyclosporine, the survival rates of organ transplant patients greatly improved.

All of a sudden, organ transplantation was no longer a strange and unique event. In a relatively short time, it progressed from an experimental pro-cedure to an accepted form of treatment for patients

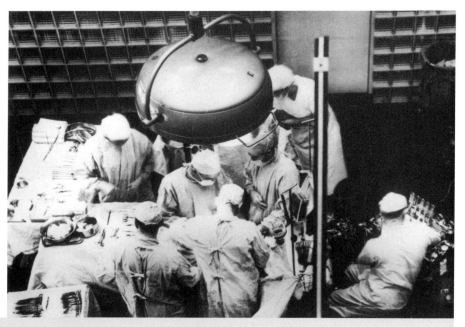

In 1990, Dr. Joseph Murray won the Nobel Prize for his work, which included the first successful kidney transplant surgery from a living donor, shown here.

who were dying from organ failure. The number of transplants multiplied greatly during the last quarter of the twentieth century. Immunologists continued to find newer and better medications that could prevent the immune system from rejecting new organs. At the same time, physicians perfected methods of removing and transplanting tissue. Finally, a variety of researchers were stirred into action by the shortage of available organs. This increased activity led to other new events.

New Ideas

In a 1966 London medical meeting, a concept called the *heart-beating cadaver* was introduced.[13] The development of ventilators and heart-lung machines could now keep the heart beating in a deceased patient. It was decided to allow physicians to pronounce a person dead when all the functions of the brain and brain stem stopped without any possibility of being started again. In 1968, the Harvard Medical School provided specific medical criteria for physicians to use to determine brain death. This allowed a person's heart to be kept artificially beating until the organs could be surgically removed for transplantation. It was now possible to procure many organs from a single donor.

The necessity of matching a person's basic blood type for transfusions had been understood for years. Dr. Paul Terasaki of the University of California at Los Angeles became one of the world's foremost authorities on a procedure called *tissue typing*. He perfected a method that detected the antigens that triggered an immune reaction.[14] Tissue matching for compatibility became a standard practice for kidney transplantation.

Between 1954 and 1973, about 10,000 kidney transplants were performed.[15] It became clear that the supply of organs could not meet the increasing demand for them. Someone had to decide who would be first in line to receive an organ from the inadequate supply. In 1984, the United States government set up a national organ procurement and distribution system with the responsibility of locating available organs and determining who would get them. In 1986, the contract for this responsibility was given to the United Network for Organ Sharing.[16]

Meanwhile, additional body parts were being transplanted for the first time. Although Dr. Richard Lillehei first described a possible procedure for a bowel transplant in 1958, he died in 1981 without seeing his operation actually used successfully on humans. Lillehei and Dr. William Kelly from the University of Minnesota performed the first successful human pancreas transplant in 1966. The first successful lung transplant was performed in Canada in 1983 by Dr. Joel Cooper.

The growth of activity in transplantation increased the search for new and better drugs. Those drugs needed to allow the body to accept donor organs while keeping the immune system healthy enough to hold back infection and disease. The Food and Drug Administration (FDA) approved several new drugs after 1960. Antithymocyte Globulin, made from horse serum, is helpful in allowing other drugs to be used in lower, less toxic doses.[17] FK506, or tacrolimus, was developed by Fujisawa Pharmaceutical Corporation. It comes from a fungus found in Japanese soil at the foot of Tsukuba Mountain.[18] It works in a similar way to cyclosporine. Cellcept began to replace Imuran in 1996 because it worked longer before producing toxic side effects.[19] Monoclonal antibodies such as OKT-3 are specially engineered in a laboratory to target certain cells and stop their attack. Thymoglobulin and Rapamune were drugs approved in 1999.[20]

Early attempts at transplanting animal organs into humans, called *xenotransplantation*, had dated as far back as 1905. Interest was revived after scientists gained further understanding of the immune system and after immunosuppressive drugs became available. The famous case was the baboon-to-human heart given to a baby named Fae by the media in 1984. Baby Fae was born with a malformed heart. She died twenty-one days after the operation. However, it appeared that the heart itself had not been rejected. Animal-to-human transplantation continued to fail and would have to wait for new and different antirejection treatment.[21]

Chimerism

In 1992, there was a study of kidney and liver recipients who over time had good function of their donated organs. The study showed that leukocytes (white blood cells) from the donor organs had migrated to different parts of the recipients' bodies. These cells had survived without being rejected in all the patients for up to thirty years. In fact, researchers found that the donor and recipient cells were peacefully coexisting in the recipients' bodies.[22] That showed that genetic material from a donor, brought in through the transplanted organ, could actually take root in a recipient's body. This is called *chimerism* after the Greek beast made out of many

The Chimera was a monster from Greek mythology with body parts from several different animals: the head of a lion, the body of a goat, and the tail of a serpent. The term "chimerism" refers to the movement of cells from donor organs to other parts of the recipient's body.

body parts.[23] Could it be possible that a woman applying lipstick was actually touching the cells of the person who had donated an organ to her thirty years before?[24]

Researchers decided that this information might help explain why some transplants are more successful or tolerated by the recipient. It might also be the reason why some patients seem to function without large amounts of immunosuppressants. It appears that donor leukocyte chimerism sometimes occurs after organ transplantation. There is some development of evidence that this is a basis for the acceptance of a new organ.[25] If it were possible to successfully recreate this process in all transplant patients, there would be less need for a lifetime of reliance on drug therapy.

Transplantation has come full circle from Greek mythology. The Chimera has given its name to a process of placing body parts from one person into another in order to save a life. The most successful outcome of that process results in the genetic material from both people mingling to produce a "chimera" effect within the recipient's body. This miracle of modern science has changed the certainty of death for those suffering from end-stage organ disease. Our present ability to transplant organs successfully is rooted in a series of major medical advances and a comprehensive understanding of the human immune system. It continues to raise questions that will be addressed in the scientific world of the twenty-first century.

3

Precious Organs

People who live with failing organs understand what it means to live under the "shadow of death." It is true that organ transplant success depends on advanced medical tools and skills. However, the most complex, sophisticated, and powerful piece in the process is the human organ itself. Organs are not manufactured, but grown. No technology compares in complexity to the workings of a human liver or kidney. Humans are given the organs they need at birth to sustain them for a lifetime. These incredible systems provide vital functions and support

36

life. They grow and adapt over time. And they protect the body with the fierceness of a thousand armies.

Disease and circumstance can cause organs to fail. Fifty years ago, a person died from the loss of an organ. It is a new medical reality that failing organs can be replaced with those from another person's body. But obtaining an organ is not an everyday event. Patients have to be near death with a failing organ to be considered as candidates to receive a new organ. If they are lucky, they will find a donor and have a successful transplant. But they will still have a long convalescence and take expensive medications for the rest of their lives.

Some recipients resume a normal lifestyle. Many can return to work, play sports, and travel. But often recipients have episodes of illness. Many spend time in the hospital when their body tries to reject the new organ. Some people have uncomfortable side effects from medication. Life may not ever be perfectly normal. But the alternative is death.

Marla's Story

The story of Marla and Steve Morrow is a wonderful example of the miracle of organ donation. Marla was diagnosed with Type 1 diabetes when she was seven years old. Her pancreas was unable to produce the insulin necessary to sustain her body's needs. At age thirty-one, her kidneys started to fail as a result of the disease. This is called renal failure. She began seeing a kidney specialist. He suggested that she might have two years before her kidneys failed altogether. Marla could not live without her kidneys.

The bean-shaped kidneys come in pairs and are located at the back of the abdomen. They are each about the size of a fist. They are embedded in a mass of fat that cushions and protects them. The kidneys perform many vital and complex functions. They are the body's filter system. They shed waste products, conserve nutrients, and regulate the blood pressure.

Marla gave her doctor permission to register her name on the waiting list for a new kidney at the University of Washington Medical Center. She then began dialysis on an artificial kidney machine. The machine took over the function of her diseased organs. Dialysis is a treatment that purifies the blood for the failing kidneys. There are two types of dialysis. Marla was on peritoneal dialysis. Her blood was cleaned inside her body through a tube placed in the abdomen. During the treatment, fluid is placed in the peritoneum, or the membrane lining the abdomen. Then the fluid is drawn out again, removing waste products from the blood.[1] After training, Marla was able to do this at home. This was fortunate because she was on dialysis for forty minutes, four times a day, seven days a week. At first, it was uncomfortable because of the amount of fluid put into her body. But she soon got used to it. Although people can live for years on dialysis, it often serves as a bridge to getting a transplant.

As her disease progressed, a good day for Marla was extremely limited. She would get out of bed and do her dialysis. Then she would test her blood sugar and blood pressure. She might have enough strength to garden for ten minutes. Then she would lie down and rest for a half hour. And she would repeat this process over again. On a bad day, she would do the dialysis and testing and go back to bed. But she had to get up and do it all over again a few hours later. Dialysis consumed her life. She found herself getting more and more depressed. The doctors were pleased with her physical progress. But Marla thought her lifestyle was unacceptable.

She became desperate. She had been on the transplant list for two years and had been called twice. The first time, she was awakened in the middle of the night. There was a kidney available. She went immediately to the hospital and had her blood drawn. The blood was rushed two hours away by taxi to the Seattle hospital for tissue matching. She went back home and waited frantically by the phone to hear the results. She had mixed feelings. She was elated because she might be close to receiving a kidney. She was also sad. She knew that if a kidney was available, some family was dealing with the pain of losing a loved one. The disappointing call came the next morning. The kidney had gone to another recipient who had been waiting longer than Marla. She was happy for the person who got the kidney, but she felt sad to be back on the list. She walked out by her horse barn and played in the dirt. She knew she could not do that after receiving a transplant because of the danger of infection. She now looks back at this time as a dress rehearsal.

The second time that Marla was called was not so

dramatic. It involved an important decision. The doctor admitted that the donor organ was not a great match for her. She had the opportunity to accept or reject the kidney. After talking it over with her doctor, she thought for a moment, prayed, and decided to reject the offer.

The Transplant Operation

Marla's husband, Steve, decided that he needed to do something. The process of dialysis was keeping Marla barely alive. It was very difficult to see the person he loved deteriorate daily. Once before, he had offered to donate one of his kidneys. At the time Marla had been considering both a kidney and a pancreas transplant. Now she had decided on a kidney alone. Steve called and talked to the transplant surgeon at the University of Washington Medical Center. "I want to do this!" he said. The doctor thought it might be possible if Marla was willing. Steve knew that getting a kidney from a living donor was a definite advantage. There would be little waiting. The kidney could be transferred from him to Marla almost immediately. This would cut down the preservation time when the kidney might deteriorate.

Steve began a series of tests the next morning. He knew their similar type O blood would be well matched. The initial screening went well. Preliminary testing took three weeks. No one questioned his motives. He and Marla had been married for twenty-five years. He wanted her to live and have the quality of life she deserved. Steve and Marla realized that

Marla Morrow, whose diabetes was causing kidney failure, received a new kidney from her husband, Steve.

the chances were slim that they would be compatible. But the University called and gave them the exciting news. They had a tissue match. Could they be ready for surgery in three weeks?

On May 23, 1999, Steve went into the operating room at 6:00 A.M. It took five hours to complete the surgery. Marla followed at 7:00 A.M. Steve's kidney was removed. Then it was rinsed and cleansed for one-half hour before transplantation. Marla's operation took three hours. The doctors placed Steve's kidney in her lower right abdomen. They left both of her own kidneys in her body. They will eventually shrivel up from nonuse. At the time of surgery, Steve was forty-eight years old and Marla was forty-six. Four days after surgery, they walked out of the hospital hand in hand.

Living With the New Kidney

Marla had to return to the hospital for a few days because she had been released too early. While there, she had a sudden longing for vanilla ice cream and Starbucks' coffee. This was food she usually did not enjoy. She left her room and located both in the hospital. Marla called Steve immediately. She was laughing about her sudden and strange cravings. He confessed that he was just on the way to the freezer to get some vanilla ice cream to eat with his cup of coffee. They wondered if Marla had gotten some of Steve's appetites along with his kidney.

Steve and Marla are lucky. Their medical costs were covered. A federal program called Medicare provides funds for kidney dialysis and transplants. Steve's colleagues at work donated sick leave to cover his five weeks' absence. Marla was told to expect at least two episodes of rejection. She has had none. She religiously sticks to her medical routine that includes a heavy schedule of drugs that suppress her immune system. These immunosuppressants keep her body from rejecting the new organ. Even with medical insurance, the drugs she takes, including FK506, Cellcept, and her diabetes medications, cost $300 a month. Without insurance, they would cost $680 a month. That cost is down from $1,500 the first few months following surgery.

Marla's new kidney is working well. She named it Rose, because roses are a symbol of love. She feels that she has been reborn. She rides her horses and has no physical restrictions. She still has diabetes, however, and that will cause the new kidney to deteriorate over time. So she is considering an islet cell transplant that will have the potential to treat her diabetes. She said, "Once you have been given a gift of life from someone who loves you, it is a big responsibility. It would be awful if I didn't take care of it."

Steve and Marla went to the same Transplant Games as the Schofields. It was heartwarming for Marla to see all the athletes who had been critically ill with organ failure. Now they were alive and well enough to compete in physically strenuous activities. She commented, "We all looked so normal!" Steve walked into the stadium with the live donors and donor families. He was overwhelmed by the standing

At the Transplant Games, Steve Morrow and other organ donors received medals honoring their gift.

ovation from thousands of athletes and recipients who were so grateful to their donors for their chance to live. He said, "It was the best thing I have ever done in my life."[2]

Currently, in the United States, there are over 80,000 persons living with a functioning kidney transplant. Hundreds of thousands of patients have received kidneys.[3] Most kidney transplants come from donors who have died, or cadavers. Public education programs aimed at increasing the number of donors have been successful. In the past several years, there has been a 20 to 30 percent increase in the number of kidneys from living donors.[4] Over five thousand persons in the United States donated a kidney in the year 2000.

The Heart

More than one hundred years ago, L. Frank Baum wrote *The Wizard of Oz*. In the original book, Dorothy meets a Tin Woodman. He explains to her that he has lost his heart through the mean enchantments of the Wicked Witch of the East. He decides to go with Dorothy and her friends to ask the great Wizard of Oz for a new heart. Part of the charm of this delightful book is that readers understand that it is only a fairy tale. Little did the author know that the day would actually come when it was possible to get a new heart.

Two-year-old Anthony Milam will someday understand exactly how the Tin Woodman felt. He received a new heart on January 19, 2001. Two months before, he had been diagnosed with severe congestive heart failure. The same illness had taken the lives of his two siblings. He was one of the youngest heart transplant patients at Children's Hospital in Seattle, Washington.[5]

Anthony would have died without a new heart. The heart is a strong and muscular organ. It pumps blood throughout the body. In an adult, it is about the size of a fist and weighs less than one pound. It is located between the lungs and slightly to the left of the breastbone. The heart is enclosed by a thin protective sac made of tough tissue. The heart is responsible for delivering oxygen and nutrients to all of the body's cells. It removes the waste products of cellular metabolism. The heart is intricately involved with all other systems in the body.

The first heart transplant astonished the entire world. For most cultures, the heart is more than an organ of the body. It is deeply symbolic. The idea of giving one's heart as a symbol of love is found in ancient and modern poetry. It has deep roots in mythical lore. The heart is believed to be the center of passion. The idea of cutting a heart out of a body touched upon a deep core of beliefs. It stirred images far beyond the simple slicing of a few veins or arteries. The heart is also a more critical organ. You can live with one kidney. You may even be able to live with a partial liver or one lung. But you have only one heart. And you cannot live without it.

The survival rate for heart transplants has improved dramatically during the last ten years. The longest surviving patient received his heart at Stanford University on January 25, 1977. He was fourteen years old. At this writing, he is still alive.

Ten percent of all heart transplants are for children.[6] At first, physicians thought that an infant's immune system would be more tolerant of a transplant than an adult's system. It was hoped that children would need fewer drugs to combat rejection. However, this has not proved true, and even newborns who receive transplants must receive immunosuppressants for the rest of their lives. Approximately 85 to

90 percent of all heart transplant patients worldwide live beyond one year. Hearts have the shortest survival time outside the donor's body. They must be transplanted within four hours.

The Liver

The liver is the largest internal organ in the body and one of the most complex. It performs more than four hundred functions each day to keep the body healthy. It is located under the right diaphragm and has four basic roles: It converts food into nutrients the body can use. It stores fats, sugars, iron, and vitamins for later use by the body. It makes proteins needed for normal blood clotting. It also removes or chemically changes drugs, alcohol, and other substances that may be harmful or toxic to the body.[7] The liver can be destroyed by an excessive use of alcohol or naturally occurring genetic disorders.

The liver is one of the most difficult and complex organs to transplant. The loss of blood during liver surgery was a problem until Thomas Starzl developed a machine called the *Veno veno bypass*. This machine keeps blood flowing in a way that gives surgeons more stability.[8]

One of the most famous liver transplant patients at this writing is twenty-nine-year-old Chris Klug from Aspen, Colorado. Chris won the bronze medal in the snowboarding giant slalom in the 2002 U.S. Winter Olympics in Utah. He became an Olympic medalist just eighteen months after receiving a liver transplant.

Snowboarder Chris Klug won a bronze medal at the 2002 Winter Olympics less than two years after his liver transplant.

On November 27, 1989, a Texan named Teri Smith became the first living related liver donor in the United States. She donated a portion of her liver to her twenty-one-month-old daughter, Alyssa, who was suffering from a fatal liver disease. This "split liver" technique has since been used with adults with good results. In 1999, Alyssa appeared at the University of Chicago Hospital to celebrate the tenth anniversary of her surgery. She was then a healthy, active eleven-year-old sixth grader who played sports and took dance lessons.[9]

In a split liver operation, a lobe, or partial section of a donor liver, is given to a recipient. This procedure increases the possibilities for more successful liver transplants from living donors. Perhaps this will help alleviate the worldwide problem of a critical shortage of organs. In July, 2002, there were 17,543 U.S. patients waiting for new livers. There were approximately 4,500 recovered from people who had died.[10] Living donors can help to fill that gap.

The Lungs

The lungs are the organs concerned with respiration, or breathing. They are located within the chest cavity and protected by the ribs and breastbone in front and the ribs and spine at the back. The lungs bring air into contact with the blood so that oxygen can be added to the body and carbon dioxide removed. The lungs are literally the "breath of life." Lung transplantation is a relatively new therapeutic option. It has been available since the 1980s. The lung is one of the largest organs that can be transplanted. It is more susceptible to rejection than other organs are. It is also exposed to antigens in the external environment during breathing.[11]

Melanie Plagerman is a fourteen-year-old ninth grader fighting cystic fibrosis. Cystic fibrosis is a genetic disease that causes breathing and digestive problems. Melanie's body produces thick, sticky mucus that clogs her lungs. This leads to chronic lung infections. There is no cure for the disease. Melanie uses a variety of treatments to clear the mucus from her lungs. These include a machine for bronchial dilation. She puts on a vest that inflates. Then she dials a setting on the machine and it vibrates. As her body shakes, the thick mucus breaks up and unclogs the lungs. Treatment sessions last for twenty minutes.

Melanie also has allergies that compound her problem. She normally has to go to the hospital about every six weeks with infections. She is on the waiting list for a double-lung transplant at Stanford Medical Center in Palo Alto, California. At this time, Melanie's transplant is "on hold" because she is managing her disease with treatment.

Melanie has spoken to the doctors at Stanford. She knows that having a transplant is a big commitment. She will have to live near the hospital for three months. Her family will carry a cellular phone or pager. When it is time, she will be flown to San Jose, California, and taken in an ambulance to the hospital. She has four hours after the phone call to reach the hospital and be prepared for surgery. Lungs are fragile organs and must be transplanted into the recipient within four to six hours.

After Russell Schofield died, his lungs went to two recipients, because a person can survive with a single lung. This is helpful because there are many more people awaiting transplants than there are lungs available. Sometimes, two donors each give a portion of their lungs to the recipient. This surgery is less common because it involves major surgery for three people.[12]

The Pancreas and Intestines

The pancreas is a gland about the size of a fist. It is located on the back of the abdomen. It is part of the digestive system and produces the insulin that is needed to control sugar levels in the blood. Transplanting part of the pancreas from a cadaver or living donor is a treatment for diabetes. This is the disease that caused Marla Morrow to lose her kidney function. A pancreas transplant is not a cure. It does not address the problem that made the body's immune system attack the pancreas in the first place.

Scientists have developed methods for isolating the islet cells in the pancreas that are responsible for producing insulin. Much research is going into the transplantation of these cells into the liver as a treatment for diabetes. It has been difficult to find ways to keep the islet cells alive and working in the recipient's body. However, there are now reports of at least a dozen successful islet cell transplants in the United States and Canada.

In this country, the number of intestine transplants has grown over the past several years from five in 1990 to 112 in 2001. It is more common to transplant the intestines along with another organ such as the liver. In 1999, 60 percent of the transplants were placed in children.[13] On October 5, 2000, the U.S. Health Care Financing Administration (now the Centers for Medicare and Medicaid Services) decided that Medicare insurance would cover intestinal transplants. This shows that these transplants have been accepted as a standard medical procedure.

Children and Transplants

Patients under the age of eighteen are defined as pediatric patients. In 1995, they accounted for 8.2 percent of all organ transplants.[14] There is not a lower age limit for children to be listed for a transplant. Some babies have been listed for transplant before birth because they have already been diagnosed with a heart problem. Of course, medical decisions about transplanting children are left to the parents or guardians. Young children cannot be expected to understand the long-term implications of surgery.

One concern about transplanting organs into young children is that they may be at considerable risk as they grow up. The drugs they take can lower their immunity to normal childhood diseases. In actual experience, with careful drug therapy most common illnesses are tolerated. Another possible long-term financial concern is an inability to get insurance as adults.

Fourteen-year-old Melanie Plagerman is on the waiting list for a lung transplant because of her cystic fibrosis. Young patients have special needs, but they generally do well with transplants.

There are concerns that need to be addressed when teenagers receive transplants. Side effects of many immunosuppressants include physical symptoms such as weight gain or puffiness. These might cause self-conscious teens to feel embarrassed about their appearance. Also, teens enjoy asserting their independence. Some people fear that teenagers might be lax in taking their critical medications. Pediatric patients have specialized needs. However, they usually do well with organ transplants.

Tissues

Tissues of the body are also used for transplantation. Corneas are the protective coverings of the eyes. Corneas have been transplanted for one hundred years because they require no protection from the immune system. (The cornea is not reached by the white blood cells of the immune system and does not react like other transplanted tissue.) There are over 40,000 cornea transplants per year in the United States.

Bone marrow is a spongy tissue found inside bones. Bone marrow contains many elements. The white blood cells fight infection. The red blood cells carry oxygen to organs and tissues and remove waste products. The platelets enable the blood to clot. Bone marrow is being used to fight a variety of diseases such as leukemia. In a bone marrow transplant, the patient's bone marrow is first destroyed through radiation. Then healthy bone marrow from a donor is infused into the patient's bloodstream. Sometimes bone marrow from a donor is transplanted along with other organs. It is hoped that it will help the recipient's immune system accept the transplant.[15] Bone marrow can come from live donors in a process that is less invasive than an operation.

Skin is a tissue that is used daily for saving the lives of burn victims. Human bones are taken from cadavers and transplanted in patients suffering from disease or accidents. The covering of the brain provides repair tissue for extensive head injuries. Ligaments, tendons, and cartilage are also transplantable tissue. Even brain cells are being used in the treatment of disease.

The idea that it was possible to transplant body parts at the beginning of the twentieth century has progressed with incredible speed. It has pushed medical boundaries beyond what was considered possible. By the end of 2010, there may be few parts of the body that have not successfully been replaced. With the advent of cloning, and the ability to isolate and reproduce cells that have particular functions in the body, the day may come where transplantation is unnecessary because a human can simply grow new cells to replace diseased organs.

4

The Immune System

Our immune system is amazingly complex. It is an effective fortress built to keep out invaders. It guards the body by keeping foreign pathogens from entering. Unbroken skin protects the body. Mucous membranes line the passages to the body's interior. Those membranes in places like the mouth and nose form a protective barrier. Tears and digestive juices high in acid also protect the body.

Inside the body, white blood cells form an army against invasion. These white blood cells, or leukocytes, originate in the body's bone marrow. They are born as stem cells. Some are called *B cells* because they mature in the bone marrow. Others go on to become *T cells* (so named because of the time they spend in the thymus gland). Finally, some become *macrophages*. These three types of cells are an army against invaders. Their strategy is clever. B cells attack by releasing antibodies that can destroy, weaken, or neutralize the enemy. T cells attack infected cells and destroy the intruders. Macrophages are large scavenger cells that clean up after the attack. Not only do these cells take care of the enemies, they also have a long memory. After they have once encountered invading pathogens, they will recognize them again and again. This memory allows them to be on guard for another possible invasion. Next time, their line of defense will be sharp and quick.

Antigens are molecules on the surface of all cells. They are proteins that stimulate the production of antibodies when introduced into a body. Antibodies are also proteins. Their production is directed by the DNA contained in a person's chromosomes. Antibodies are responsible for attacking and neutralizing antigens. They produce immunity against those antigens. This is the basic problem faced by organ transplant recipients. Foreign antigens from transplanted organs will trigger an immune response. That stimulates the production of antibodies to launch an attack when an organ is transplanted into a new body.

The immune system is immediately available in time of need. It reacts against viruses and infections.

A fever, for instance, announces the increased rate of the immune system's reaction. It speeds the movement of the army of white blood cells to the source of the infection. The increase in the body's temperature itself may help to kill foreign pathogens. The memory cells guard against a second invasion. They immediately recognize an infection and keep it from taking hold in the body a second time. This is the reason that a person does not contract some diseases twice. It is the principle behind immunizations. Vaccines can be injected into the body to protect it from diseases such as measles, mumps, and polio. Infants are protected from infections by the antibodies they receive from their mothers before birth and after birth through breast milk.

The Immune Barrier

Peter Medawar began describing the immune system in the 1940s during the Second World War. He observed how patients rejected foreign skin grafted on to their bodies. He won the Nobel Prize in Medicine in 1960 for his work. He was the first to understand how the immune system fought off any substance that it identified as foreign or not related to it. He understood that the surface of each separate cell represented a particular chemical pattern distinctive to the individual. Those cells of the body that fought against foreign substances promptly recognize the unique pattern of cells in the invading tissue. Their job is to detect what is related or not related to the body itself.

In describing the human immune system, Dr. Peter Medawar produced the century's most important breakthrough in the field of transplantation. He received the Nobel Prize in Physiology or Medicine in 1960.

Sir Frank Macfarlane Burnet received a Nobel Prize the same year as Dr. Peter Medawar. Burnet thought that the central problem was how the tissues in the body sorted out those substances that could be categorized as "self" and those that were foreign and "not self." A person's immune pattern is part of his or her genetic makeup. However, the capacity to fully recognize and remember the "self" develops weeks or months after birth. This fact was important later when fooling the immune system became the goal of transplant physicians. Medawar's studies with mice showed that tolerance might be built into the immune system. He injected cells from a foreign substance into a fetus before birth. He wanted to cause those cells to grow and become a natural part of the body so that they would not be rejected.[1]

The body's superior defenses that resist foreign substances were the barrier to successful organ transplantation. The good news was that the immune system kept humans alive and healthy. Now, it suddenly became a problem. After the first transplants, it was clear just how much of a problem or barrier that good news was to the field of organ transplants. The bad news was that virtually none of the first transplants worked because the human body was successful in eliminating intruders.

The first trials at fooling the immune system with radiation and drugs simply wiped out the body's ability to protect itself. They left the body completely defenseless against invading organisms. This certainly was not acceptable. One might have a successful transplant surgery, only to die of an infection a short time later. It was not until the discovery of cyclosporine that an agent was found that would leave some of the immune system intact. But even that drug had serious side effects that were detrimental to the body. There has been great progress with drugs that suppress the immune system in the last twenty-five years. However, scientists are still searching for better ways to keep the immune system healthy and functioning against disease while allowing it to accept a foreign tissue or organ. Experiments with adjusting the combinations and levels of drugs have produced the best results to date. Many diseases, such as arthritis, multiple sclerosis, and diabetes, are related to the immune system. The use of new drugs and the manipulation of the cells of the body may well have a positive medical impact far beyond the benefits to organ transplantation.

Tests to Determine Compatibility

There are several tests that can be performed on donor organs or on living donors to help determine the compatibility between the donor's and recipient's immune systems. The object is to try to minimize the more devastating effects of rejection. Blood typing is a laboratory test done to determine the antigens found on the surface of the red blood cells. Dr. Karl Landsteiner received the 1930 Nobel Prize in Medicine for his discovery of blood typing. Blood typing has been used for years to regulate the safety of blood transfusions. People have O, A, B, or AB blood types. If you have type A blood, your blood cells contain the A antigen. If you have type B blood, your cells contain the B antigen. AB blood contains both A and B antigens. However, O blood contains neither A or B antigens. Blood is also tested for a particular antigen named the D antigen. If the D antigen is present in the blood, a person is Rh-positive. If it is absent, the person is Rh-negative.[2] It is critically important that the donor organ's blood type is compatible with the recipient's blood type. If it is not, the body will immediately produce antibodies against the antigens. It will reject the transplant.

A cross match test can show if the recipient has previously developed antibodies that will react against the donor organ. In a cross match, a small amount of the prospective recipient's blood is mixed with white blood cells from the possible donor. If there is a reaction, the cross match is positive. The donor and recipient are not compatible. A negative cross match means there is no reaction. The transplant may proceed. This test is called *percent reactive antibody* (PRA). It represents the percentage of the population to which a recipient is likely to have a positive cross match. Someone with a PRA of 50, for example, is likely to be sensitized to organs from 50 percent of the population.[3] Sometimes earlier conditions cause a sensitized immune system. Such things as previous organ transplants, blood transfusions, viruses, or pregnancy might signal the white memory cells to immediately attack foreign cells.

White blood cell antigens or human leukocyte antigens (HLA antigens) are inherited from parents. They can also be tested before a transplant operation.

It is important to find as close a match between donor and recipient as is possible through tissue typing. A match may be desirable, but it is not completely necessary. Three groups important for transplantation (named HLA-A, HLA-B, HLA-DR antigens) are inherited from each parent. However, each particular group contains a variety of individual antigens. The possibility of finding exactly the right combination to match another person who is not a blood relative is rare.[4]

Statistics have shown that higher levels of HLA matching may lead to longer survival times. But because of the effectiveness of newer drugs, the difference is not overwhelming.

In addition to blood typing, cross matching, and tissue typing, there are other factors taken into consideration when matching a donor organ to a recipient. These may include the organ's condition, the size of the organ, and the ability to move the organ from one geographic location to another in a reasonable amount of time. Other considerations include how sick the prospective recipient is and how long he or she has waited for a new organ.

Rejection

Rejection happens when the body identifies the donated organ as an invader and attacks it. Everything possible is done to keep the new organ from being rejected. Testing helps in advance. However, fragile organs removed from a person who is brain dead might need to be transplanted before

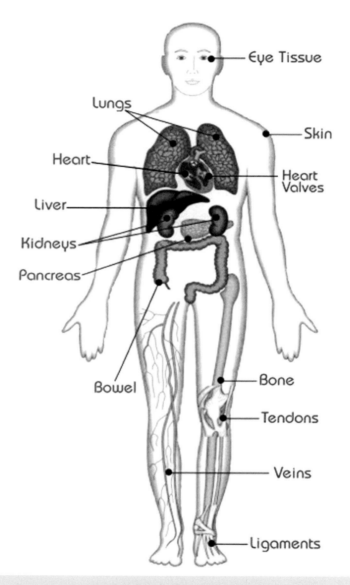

Transplantable organs of the human body

some tests can be completed. HLA matching, for instance, is used mainly for kidneys. The time factor for transplanting kidneys is not as critical as that for transplanting the heart or lungs. HLA matching can best be used with living donors where there is time enough for the testing to be set up in advance of the operations.

There are three principal kinds of rejection to transplanted organs. In hyperacute rejection, the recipient has a large number of antibodies that react immediately against the donor organ. It may be that the immune system already has been sensitized toward the donor or the blood types were not compatible. The rejection is quick and immediate. However, because of the antibody screening, this type of rejection is rarely seen.

Acute rejection may happen within weeks or even years after the transplant. First, it takes several days for the immune system's T cells to recognize the new organ as foreign. Then, immunosuppressive drugs are used to prevent acute rejection. If the drugs were not used, virtually all transplanted organs would be rejected within two weeks.[5] Often patients have one or more episodes of acute rejection that are treated with antirejection drugs.

Chronic rejection takes place over a long period of time. It is the most common cause of organ loss. It seems to be caused by a slow deterioration of the donor organ despite increased doses of immunosuppression.[6] Rejection can work both ways. When the recipient's body forms antibodies against the donor organ, it causes a disease called Host Versus Graft or

HVG. But the opposite can also happen. The new organ's immune cells can attack the recipient body in a dangerous condition called Graft Versus Host disease or GVHD.

It is sometimes difficult to tell the difference between an infection that might be aided with fewer drugs and an episode of rejection. The rejection might need higher doses of immunosuppression. Some ways of detecting rejection early enough to treat it are ultrasounds, blood analysis, and the use of biopsies that remove tissue from the transplanted organ.

Immunosuppression

Keeping the body from rejecting a new organ has been the major goal of the medical community since transplantation began. Patient survival rates have increased dramatically over the years. Part of the success is due to the increased understanding of organ failure and improved patient care before and after surgery. Other reasons for success include a better understanding of the immune system and the attempt to match the donor organ to the recipient to prevent hyperacute rejection. It is clear that tremendous resources and energy have gone toward the research and development of drugs that act as immunosuppressive agents.

In order to halt or prevent rejection, organ transplant patients rely on the most advanced drugs in existence to suppress the natural activities of the immune system. But immunosuppressive drugs are of primitive simplicity compared to the organs they are used to protect.[7] During the past ten years, several new drugs that work more specifically have been approved for use. The increased selection has provided physicians with a large supply of antirejection drugs. It has allowed them to develop different strategies and combinations to fit particular patients. Unfortunately, all of the immunosuppressants have serious side effects. These vary from drug to drug. After the initial high doses following surgery, each patient works with the physician to find a combination that will protect the transplant from rejection with a minimum amount of drug therapy. Episodes of

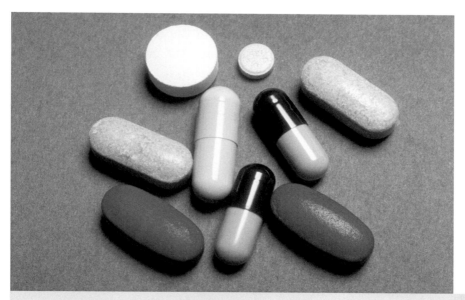

Today, scientists are engineering drugs to target specific cells in the effort to reduce rejection of transplanted organs.

rejection mean high emergency doses of antirejection drugs. Smaller doses are needed to maintain the transplant over a longer period of time. Fortunately, new drugs are being created that have the potential to be taken less frequently with fewer side effects.

Physicians have had some success by transplanting bone marrow along with an organ.[8] The hope is that the bone marrow will produce white blood cells and create a state of chimerism. This state would blend the immune systems of the donor and the recipient and increase the tolerance to organ transplants. Without a doubt, the advances in the field of immunosuppression are responsible for today's success in the field of organ transplantation. One could look at explosion in the sheer numbers of patients on the waiting list. The growth in the field is the result of the ability to use transplantation as a medical cure for patients who previously would have died from the loss of one of their organs.

5

The Business of Organ Transplants

In 1963, there were 244 human organ transplants reported worldwide. Only nine transplant recipients had survived for more than one year. From 1988 to 1998, the annual number of solid organ transplants increased 71 percent. They went from 12,789 to 21,926 in the United States alone.[1] The field of transplantation took off at rocket speeds. The demand for organs far exceeded the supply. This created a national dilemma of major proportions.

Organ transplantation in the United States depended upon several factors coming together. First was the development of medical technologies. As the field grew, government support was needed in terms of financing and laws. A nationwide structure to locate donors and categorize recipients regulated the supply and demand of organs. Finally, citizens acted generously and agreed that organs should be freely donated. In a real sense it is the blending of technology and human kindness that makes organ transplantation possible.[2]

The supply and demand of organs in the United States is public business. Government involvement has greatly increased over the years. This is due to public awareness of organ transplantation and the symbolic issues arising from the use of human organs. By improving the effectiveness of the way organs are obtained and distributed, the government could increase the supply of organs.[3] There was a need for new laws. There was also a need for organizational structures across the country to handle the distribution of organs. Assistance was necessary to cover the enormous financial costs of transplantation. Government regulations and funding make the entire infrastructure of organ procurement and distribution possible.

Statistics

Today, according to data from UNOS, a new name is added to the national organ waiting list every eighteen minutes. In July 2002, there were over 80,000 patients in the United States waiting for a life-giving organ. During 2001, a total of 24,076 organs were transplanted from 12,580 donors. About half of the donors were cadavers. The rest were living donors.[4] The number of organs donated always exceeds the number of donors. Like Russ Schofield, one donor can provide organs for several people. In 2001, there were 6,124 people on the waiting list who died before an organ became available.[5]

Organ transplantation is not just one treatment of choice for most people dying from end-stage disease. It is becoming more acceptable as a lifesaving medical procedure. An increasing number of people are registered. The scarcity of available organs grows yearly. It has been suggested that there might be approximately 14,000 potential cadaver organ donors annually in this country. But donation is voluntary in the United States. It is a private decision. It cannot be compensated. That is, organs cannot be bought or sold in America.

Most decisions to donate cadaver organs are made by mothers, fathers, children, and siblings of the deceased person. Unfortunately, those critical decisions have to be made while the family is in the midst of dealing with tragedy. It is amazing that so many persons in the past have reached out to help one or more strangers during such a private moment. Families of donors are not able to choose the recipient. They might not know who receives the organs.

A person can indicate a willingness to donate an organ on a driver's license. However, even if a person has indicated this, his or her family may disagree, and the hospital and organ procurement organization are reluctant to ignore the wishes of the family members who are present. Hospitals request written consent before organs are removed for transplant.[6] Because time is such a critical factor, families must be provided with information about the opportunity to donate their loved one's organs even in the midst of their tragedy.

A Critical Shortage

The supply of cadaver donors has not changed significantly over the years compared to the increased demand for organs. Because of this, living donors have assumed an increased importance. There are several advantages to using living donors. Statistics show that transplanted organs from living donors do better. Recipients do not have to wait until an organ is available. They can plan in advance. Most

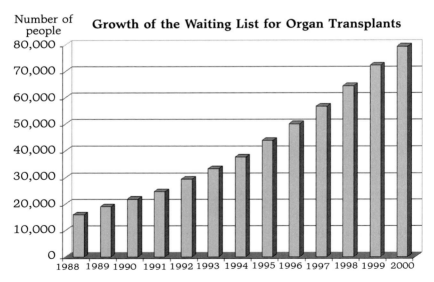

Source: Transplant Patient Data Source, *United Network for Organ Sharing Online*, February 28, 2002, <http://www.patients.unos.org/tpd> (July 25, 2002).

important, the organ is not out of the donor's body too long. It does not have to be transported to another location. There is an increase in using living donors. However, giving away an organ is a serious commitment. Living donors cannot give away organs that compromise their own lives. A living donor, for instance, cannot give away a heart.

Not all people who die are possible donors. Organs begin to deteriorate immediately after death. This is especially true of victims of multiple gunshots and those who have died in automobile accidents without being placed on life support. Interestingly, traffic fatalities in the United States have decreased over the years. This is due to seatbelt laws, a higher minimum drinking age, and stronger enforcement of drunk driving laws. In 1986, perhaps 45 percent of all organ donors died as a result of motor vehicle accidents. In 1990, only 25 percent did.[7] The age and physical health of potential donors are taken under consideration. For instance, in most cases, an organ would not be used if the donor has AIDS, for fear of spreading the disease. However, on occasion, an HIV-positive patient has donated to an HIV-positive recipient.

According to the National Transplant Society, more than 85 percent of the people in the United States approve of organ donation. Yet only 35 percent say they would actually donate organs. Several ideas have been suggested to increase the number of available donor organs. Public education through the media may encourage people to donate their own organs or those of a loved one. Increasing the maximum age of donors and taking organs from donors in less than optimum health have worked better than was originally expected. The 1998 Conditions of Participation mandates that every potential donor's family be given the most complete and up-to-date information by the nearest organ procurement agency. This should show results over time.

Other ideas suggest changing the laws about organ donation. One thought is to offer a financial benefit to donor families in the form of tax credits or payments toward funeral expenses. Another idea is to adopt the very controversial European "presumed consent" laws. These laws dictate that physicians presume that donation is allowed. They take the organs from a cadaver unless the person or family specifically says no.[8] The government could make the wishes expressed on a driver's license mandatory and incapable of being overridden. There are researchers who believe that utilizing animal organs or cloning human organs will fill the gap between the supply and demand for organs to transplant.

The Laws

The United States organ procurement system is the largest in the world by a substantial margin. It is impressive for its size and for its rate of growth. As the field of organ transplantation grew during the second half of the twentieth century, most states put together a variety of regulations about the subject. In 1968 the federal government passed the Uniform

Anatomical Gift Act. It was eventually accepted by all fifty states with variations provided by individual legislatures. This act resulted in the wallet-sized donor card. When the card is signed by a person over eighteen and witnessed by two other adults, it is a legal instrument permitting physicians to remove organs after death.[9] However, as stated earlier, in practice, family consent is required for organ donation to occur.

The National Organ Transplant Act of 1984 was brought about by the shortage of donor organs. This act funded a national system of private organ procurement organizations (OPOs). It also established the United Network for Organ Sharing as the Organ Procurement and Transplantation Network. UNOS would assist the OPOs in the distribution of organs throughout the country. A provision of the act specifically forbids payment for organ donation.[10] The act also created a twenty-five-member task force to study a variety of policy issues. These issues included how organs were procured and distributed in the United States.

One of the concerns of the task force was to find its way into the Omnibus Budget Reconciliation Act of 1986. The act required all hospitals participating in federal funding to have a "required request" policy. That meant that hospitals were responsible to identify potential donors. They were also responsible to give families information about organ and tissue donation as well as their option to decline.

In 1998, Vice President Al Gore and Donna Shalala, Secretary of the U.S. Department of Health

Fragile organs are cooled and placed in a sterile container and then swiftly transported to waiting recipients, often by airplane. Organs can survive for only a limited time away from their blood supply.

and Human Services, launched the National Organ and Tissue Donation Initiative. From this initiative came new regulations aimed at saving lives by substantially increasing organ donation in the United States. As a condition for participating in the Medicare reimbursement program, hospitals are required to notify an organ procurement organization of all people who are near death or who have died. The organ procurement organization takes the responsibility for identifying all potential donors. They give families information about organ and tissue donation. They also inform families about their option to decline.

Organizational Structure

The United Network for Organ Sharing in Virginia has the federal contract to manage the growing national transplant waiting list. UNOS membership includes hospital transplant centers and organ procurement organizations. These organ procurement centers are the regional centers responsible for the actual coordination of the donations. UNOS maintains the database of patients accepted onto a transplant program's waiting list. The computer program contains patient lists ranked according to medical criteria. These include blood type, tissue type, size of organ, and medical urgency. The program also indicates the time spent on the waiting list and the distance between the donor and the transplant center.

UNOS continues to collect, assemble, and maintain transplant data on donors and recipients. In 2000,

URREA (the University Renal Research and Education Association) was awarded the Scientific Registry of Transplant Recipients contract to perform the analyses that measure the efficiency and fairness of transplantation. This data is used to improve the medicine and science of transplantation. It also will help develop organ allocation policy, aid scientific research, and support transplant professionals in caring for patients. The OPOs, the Coalition on Donation, and the individual transplant centers raise public awareness about the importance of organ donation. They work to keep patients informed about transplant issues and policy.

The local OPO does the actual work of coordinating the donation. The OPO is informed by the hospital that a potential donor is dead or dying. The OPO then communicates with prospective donor families. It is important to understand that members of the hospital staff concerned with saving a life and responsible for notifying the family about a death are completely separate from members of the organ procurement staff.

The OPO is in charge of the medical management of the donor organs. It coordinates medical teams to retrieve organs. It accesses the UNOS computer data and enters information about the donor organs. It runs the tissue match program. It is responsible for the distribution of organs. Some organs may be transported hundreds of miles to a transplantation center. Others have a short preservation time and must be used by someone who lives close to the donor. The law requires the OPOs to have a system for allocating organs to patients equitably. This system is based upon established medical criteria. The OPO also provides training for healthcare professionals in hospitals. It assists hospitals in carrying out their legal obligation to refer potential donors.[11]

The Waiting List

A patient must be referred by a physician to get placed on the waiting list for an organ transplant. There is a growing shortage of donor organs. There are also a large number of people in need of transplant surgery. These facts increase the pressure to select patients most likely to benefit from the surgery. Each hospital has an evaluation team. The evaluation or screening includes medical tests and interviews with people. The teams determine a patient's ability to handle the physical and mental strain of the transplantation. The teams gather information about a patient's support system. They will assess the use of drugs or alcohol and the patient's ability to comply with the rigid expectations of a lifetime of drug therapy. In general, the sickest patients with the least time to live and the most limited physical capacity move to the top of the list. Patients with fewer lifestyle restrictions and with the ability to wait longer are given lower priority.[12]

Hospitals must also assess the patient's ability to pay. Organ transplantation is exceedingly expensive for recipients even though organs are donated. A liver transplant alone may cost from $150,000 to $300,000. Even a relatively simple kidney transplant can end up costing close to $100,000 with all the related expenses before and after surgery.[13] These expenses do not cover the cost of immunosuppressive drugs. Those drugs can easily reach $7,000 per year. And they must be taken for life.[14]

Paying for a Transplant

How do people pay such expenses? Some cannot. Others pay in a variety of ways. In 1972, Congress authorized payment for patients on dialysis or receiving kidney transplants. At that time, Congress estimated the cost would be $140 million per year. The United States federal government now pays more than $2 billion annually to cover kidney transplants. They had no way of predicting the growth of kidney

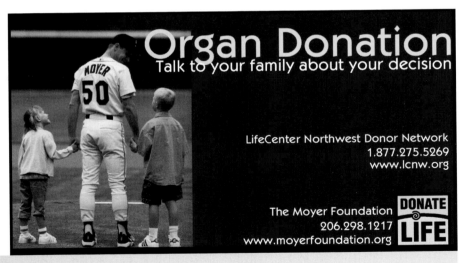

Posters are one way of encouraging the public to consider donating their own organs or those of a loved one.

transplants. The government pays through federal insurance programs such as Medicare and Medicaid. Some private and employer insurance companies cover transplants. Private foundations or nonprofit organizations may provide financial assistance. Fund-raisers sponsored by the families or friends of recipients are common. Of course, patients with the financial ability can simply pay for the transplant.

Once the patient has passed the initial screening, proven the ability to pay, and been listed on the national computer, the only thing left is to wait for an organ to become available. That sounds very simple. But remember that the person who has met these strict criteria is facing death because of a failing organ. And remember that there is an extreme shortage of organs. The question is, will the person be lucky enough to receive an organ before he or she dies?

6

The Future of Organ Transplants

Fifty years of rapid advancement in transplant medicine places high expectations on the future. It is impossible to know for certain what medical miracles the next half century will bring about. But clues can be found in recent medical trials and research.

Tremendous effort is going into possible cures for disease. The use of islet cell transplants to treat diabetes is often in the news. Nearly 200,000 people a year die of diabetes complications. These include heart disease and stroke. Diabetes is a leading cause of blindness, kidney disease, and nerve disease that leads to leg amputation. Diabetes is the result of the body's immune system attacking and destroying islet cells in the pancreas. Pancreas transplants have permitted many diabetics to stop injecting insulin. But there are not enough pancreas organs to go around. About 1,000 become available each year for transplantation.[1] It is much simpler and less invasive to transplant the islet cells themselves. However, it takes two cadaver donors to provide the 800,000 cells needed for a single transplant.

Critical problems are now being addressed. How will the cells be isolated and extracted without causing them damage? Where are the cells placed in the body to keep the immune system from destroying them? How can the cells be kept alive and replaced without frequent surgery?[2]

Islet cells are a small part of the growing list of body parts being considered for transplant. Some of the latest experiments have had mixed success. A surgeon in Germany has recently transplanted knees into five patients. Four patients recovered some degree of movement. The fifth lost her transplant due to infection.[3] In February 2001, a Kentucky gutter installer became the third person in the world to get a new hand. Two weeks before, a New Zealander had his new hand amputated when his body rejected it. He was the first hand transplant patient. An eight-year-old Mexican boy received a nerve transplant in November 2000. The next March, fetal nerve cells were transplanted into a person's brain in an attempt to control Parkinson's disease.[4] Transplantation continues to evolve as the list expands to include most parts of the body.

New Techniques

New techniques continue to be developed that may alter both the demand and supply of organs. Researchers continue their search to understand why some recipients are able to rely less on the use of expensive, and potentially damaging, immune suppressants. A variety of strategies are being developed to help the immune system to accept organ transplants. Drug researchers are trying ways to block or even deplete the genes that attack donor organs. They are also trying to modify the genes of the donor organ before transplantation.[5]

Studies are being conducted to understand how the use of bone marrow and stem cells, combined with solid organ transplantation, can sometimes produce chimerism. This allows the immune system of the donor and recipient to coexist in a way that prevents rejection of the transplanted organ by the recipient's body.

Immune suppressants have evolved from targeting cells in a more generalized fashion. They now have the ability to interfere selectively with those parts of the immune system most responsible for rejecting the donor organ. We owe much to the mapping of human genetics. The process by which drugs are developed is continually being altered. There is much less trial and error. Drugs are now being

Researchers are looking for new ways to ensure that transplanted organs are not rejected.

designed for a specific purpose. Scientists are now able to identify particular molecules that control the immune system. They can build drugs to selectively change the immune reaction. These drugs are called *monoclonal antibodies*. Some have been in use for several years. They are designed to target particular areas of the immune system specifically. They can also preserve the ability of the recipient's body to fight off infection and cancer. These are the two devastating side effects of previous immune suppressants.[6] As more research into the human genome is accomplished, researchers hope to be able to create "virtual cells" inside a computer. This will allow testing of potential drugs to take place in safety without using humans or animals as subjects.[7]

One scientist has been working on an alternative theory about the immune system. Dr. Polly Matzinger wondered why the body seemed to accept some foreign substances and not others. For instance, why does a mother's body not reject a fetus growing in its womb? She has come up with a new model. It suggests that the immune system is not alerted by the presence of foreign cells. It is alerted by the cells of the body that send out signals when they are in danger or distress. If this is correct, it might be possible to selectively block the danger signal to the immune system to keep it from rejecting the new organ.

Artificial Organs

On July 2, 2001, the world's first self-contained artificial heart was installed in Robert Tools, a fifty-

The AbioCor, an artificial heart developed in 2001, can extend the life of a recipient for a short time while the patient is waiting for a heart transplant.

year-old man. He had only a few days to live. He had been denied a heart transplant. The softball-sized plastic and titanium pump includes a rechargeable internal battery. It has a device that regulates the pumping speed. It also has an external battery that powers the artificial heart by passing electricity through the skin.[8] Tools lived almost five months with his artificial organ. He died on November 30, 2001. Artificial hearts have been around for half a century. But they were large machines. They kept patients bedridden with wires and tubes penetrating the chest to connect to a power source. The Jarvik-7 was implanted in a patient named Barney Clark in 1982. He lived for 112 miserable days. He suffered from convulsions, kidney failure, respiratory problems, and a wandering mind. Then his entire organ system failed. After that, *The New York Times* nicknamed artificial heart research the "Dracula of Medical Technology."[9]

With advances in microprocessors, biomaterials, batteries, and motors, designers have solved many problems with the newer artificial hearts. But a natural heart is not just a pump. It has a range of abilities that cannot be copied by a machine. It can pump a little or a lot of blood as the occasion requires. A resting heart pumps out five liters of blood every minute. As the heart beats faster during exercise, the output increases dramatically. A natural heart sends out chemicals to keep blood from clotting. It extracts fuel and nutrients from the blood and uses them to continuously rebuild itself. Such feats are still beyond the dreams of engineers. The artificial heart transplanted on July 2, 2001, called the AbioCor, is still an experimental device expected to extend the life of the recipient a very short time. A heart transplant with a donor organ could possibly last 15 to 30 years. Unfortunately, only half of the Americans on waiting lists received donor hearts in 2000.

The left ventricular assist device (LVAD) is a partial artificial heart that is used to boost the left ventricle's pumping action. These will help people survive until an artificial heart is available. Devices that carry over an organ until it can be transplanted are called bridges.[10] Mechanical organs are not able to replace the intricate workings of a natural human organ. Perhaps their greatest use to date is as bridges to keep people alive while organs become available.

Today, research labs contain prototypes of many body parts. The history of these efforts may be traced to Dr. Willem J. Kolff, who is known as the father of artificial organs. Dr. Kolff designed the first artificial kidney. He also developed an artificial heart in the 1950s. He formed an artificial organ research program at the University of Utah in the 1960s. In 1991, researchers developed a method of broadcasting electrical power through the skin. Artificial organs no longer need a connection through the skin to an outside power source.[11] Researchers are working on computer chips that can be implanted in the brain or spinal cord. Cochlear implants are used to help the deaf hear. There is hope that vision can be brought to the blind and speech to the victims of stroke. The bionic man or woman may be a reality during this century.

Xenotransplantation

The idea of using animals to supply body parts for humans has been known since 1905. Heart valves from pigs and blood vessels from cows had been used for years. But a better understanding of the immune system and the introduction of immunosuppressant drugs opened new possibilities in solid organ transplantation by the middle of the century. In 1963, Dr. Keith Reemtsma placed chimpanzee kidneys into six of his dying patients. All survived the surgery and one continued to live for nine months.[12] Shortly after that, one of the pioneers of surgery, Dr. James D. Hardy, who had transplanted the first human lung, transplanted the heart of a chimpanzee into the chest of a dying man. It beat 90 minutes before it stopped.[13]

The genetic makeup of larger primates is about 98 percent identical to humans. Physicians thought that a donated chimpanzee organ might function as well as a human organ from an unrelated donor would function. It might keep a person alive for a short time. However, it seemed unwise to pursue animal-to-human transplants when human-to-human transplants were not always successful. By 1984, the introduction of more effective drugs led to an attempt to give Baby Fae the baboon heart.

After the waiting list for organs grew out of proportion to the demand, scientists wanted to give the effort another try. In 1992, two baboon livers were transplanted into patients.[14] In April 1995, doctors in Massachusetts injected fetal pig brain cells into the brains of patients with advanced Parkinson's disease. And a patient in San Francisco was injected with baboon bone marrow. He was still living a year later. However, there was no evidence that the baboon cells were responsible for keeping him alive.[15]

Transplanting organs between different species is called *xenotransplantation* (*xeno* means "foreign").

Xenotransplantation is the transplanting of organs between different species. Scientists are attempting to genetically alter pig organs for transplants into humans.

The way to determine whether two creatures are of the same species is to decide whether reproduction is possible. Two animals that can mate and successfully produce offspring are considered the same species. For instance, two different breeds of dogs are the same species. But a dog and a pig are different. And, of course, humans and other animals are not the same species. This kind of transplantation has been continually tried and usually failed very rapidly.

Xenotransplantation is experimental. At this time, no one would expect to substitute an animal organ if a human organ were available. In fact, many scientists think it will never work. Others feel that it is the cutting edge of transplantation. In addition, some think that animal organs can also serve as a bridge for people who will die before a human organ transplant is possible. However, at this time animal organs are rejected by the human immune system.

Research continues on the possible use of animal organs. One concern expressed by the medical community is that animal diseases will be transmitted into the human population. "Mad cow disease" in Britain is an example of an animal virus that causes a disease in humans. Baboons and pigs have traditionally been targeted as the favored donors. Baboons are genetically close to humans, and pigs have anatomies strikingly similar to humans' in size.[16] Baboons reproduce slowly and harbor many viruses. Therefore, they are more likely to transmit disease.

The transplant community has ruled out primates for use in transplantation because many are endangered species. However, pigs are extremely easy to breed. They can produce two litters of babies a year. And pigs are slaughtered to feed humans. This might make them more acceptable to animal rights organizations to use for transplantation. Studies are being conducted on the idea of genetically modifying and then cloning pigs that would be less likely to trigger rejection in humans. In January 2002, two groups of scientists claimed they had cloned pigs whose organs lacked a genetic trait that is rejected by humans. They believe it is possible to make pig hearts and kidneys the human immune system would tolerate. In 1992 two women received pig liver transplants as bridges to hold them over until human transplants were found. Only one patient survived long enough to receive a human liver.[17]

Animals are widely used within human societies for a variety of purposes. These include providing food, clothing, companionship, and entertainment, as well as subjects for scientific research. Animal rights groups question whether humans have the right to use other species for their own purposes. Some of the concerns raised have to do with the treatment of experimental animals, the acceptability of genetically manipulating animals, and the use of particular species. As the era of genetic engineering increasingly becomes a reality, it is possible that xenotransplantation will be obsolete with the advent of cloned organs.

Cloning Organs

Neo-organs are man-made and grown from a human's own cells as a result of tissue engineering. A form of man-made skin is the first commercial product of tissue engineering. It is already on the market in the United States. Tissue-engineered cartilage should be next.[18] Scientists believe there is evidence to predict that it might be possible to engineer large, complex organs such as livers, kidneys, breasts, bladders, and intestines. All of these organs are made of many different kinds of cells.[19]

Scientists are searching for ways to grow organs and tissue within the body instead of in an artificial environment. They believe that cells can be placed in the desired site. They would be allowed to grow within their natural environment. The procedure, for instance, for repairing knee-cartilage damage is to take tissue from the patient's knee. Then the tissue is medically engineered in a laboratory. Finally, the cells are implanted into the injury. Full regeneration takes between twelve and eighteen months.[20]

Skin, bone, and cartilage are relatively simple to engineer. Cartilage, for example, has a low nutrient need and does need the growth of new blood vessels. New cartilage can even be shaped into the forms of ears and noses. Studies suggest that engineering solid organs will be more difficult. Tissue engineers are looking at the fact that livers have the unique potential to regenerate partially after injury. They have created new liver-like tissues in animals from transplanted liver cells. The new tissue growth may replace a single chemical function of the liver in animals. However, the complex functions of the organ have not been replicated.[21]

Much of the research and development is based

upon the use of embryonic stem cells. These are cells that are taken from very young human embryos grown in the laboratory. They can also be bought from fertilization clinics. This is extremely controversial. Some groups oppose this work because it results in the death of the embryo. They want to limit the research to more mature adult stem cells retrieved from the body. However, some scientists claim that adult stem cells are more difficult to grow and do not survive as long as embryonic stem cells. It remains a politically hot issue that is still being debated in the United States legislature. On July 31, 2001, the House of Representatives voted for a broad ban on human cloning. Eighty Nobel Prize winners disagree. They have signed a petition endorsing the research.[22] Political pressure on world leaders has been mounting from various interest groups who believe that stem-cell research using embryonic cells is unacceptable. They ask, "Are we destroying human life in order to advance our scientific curiosity?"[23]

In August of 2001, President George W. Bush banned the use of government money for research using stem cells from newly created embryos. He allowed the use of existing cell lines. In July 2002, his Council on Bioethics agreed that cloning for reproductive purposes should be banned outright but admitted to being divided on the issue of using human embryos for medical research. The members did not support the permanent ban favored by Bush and approved earlier by the House. But a slim majority (ten out of eighteen members) favored a four-year waiting period to allow for further debate.[24] On

September 22, 2002, Governor Gray Davis of California challenged the Bush administration and Congress by signing a law that expands stem cell research in his state. Although there was opposition within the state, the governor said he was determined to keep California at the forefront of biomedical research.

Research scientists have been worried that a national ban would allow private-sector scientists to continue cloning without supervision. However, if the current bills ever pass the Senate, no one will be able to use human embryos for cloning without receiving a penalty of up to ten years in prison and fines of one million dollars. Cloning is just one of the many controversial issues that will face organ transplantation over the next several years.

7

The Ethics of Organ Transplants

The rapid growth of organ transplantation is a global problem. The field of transplantation has its roots in medicine. However, it is at the forefront of scientific and technological research and development in the world. This has created a need for structure and laws to ensure the protection of society. Governments facing the problem of supply and demand have to ask and answer many questions. Who will get the few available organs? How should recipients be chosen? How should organs be distributed? Who should pay the fees? There are other serious issues. Should people share body parts? Is it appropriate to buy organs? Is it right to use embryos in research to develop cures for disease? Everyone who comes into contact with organ transplantation—from scientists to animal rights enthusiasts, from patients to donors, from surgeons to politicians—has a personal interest in telling their side of the story. The issues can be complicated.

The physical and financial costs of organ transplantation are high. From the beginning, patients had little chance of survival. Surgeons operated on those who were willing to grab a chance to prolong their life. But they continued to die after receiving new organs. The field was in its infancy. Medical procedures had yet to be developed. Immunologists were busy learning about the nature of the human body. They did not fully understand the process of rejection. The first people who received animal parts and artificial organs had little hope of success. They were simply medical subjects in an experimental field. Whether or not they should have been allowed to donate their lives for a medical experiment is a question of ethics. Ethics is the study of what is right or wrong.

The present success of organ transplantation is a direct result of the trial and error operations. Those operations led to the development of surgical techniques. They led to a deeper understanding of the immune system. But the question still has to be asked: Is it right to use human subjects for medical experiments? What if they are already dying? What if the chance of prolonging their life is slim? Is it taking advantage of a dying person's condition to offer a slight chance of survival? Is the possibility of saving many lives in the future worth the sacrifice of a few single lives?

Organ transplantation has evolved and has proven to be a medical option for some dying people. The demand for transplants now far exceeds the supply of available organs. The issues become even more critical. In the beginning, doctors and hospitals were completely in charge of the transplantation process. As the demand for organs increased, the government intervened. It organized structures that would handle the distribution of organs from cadavers. In recent years, the United States has decided that donated organs are public property. The organ distribution system is the public's trustee for them.[1] Because Congress allocates a sizeable portion of funds for transplantation in the United States, the debate is political. There are two key issues: Who should be eligible for a transplant, and how should the organs be distributed?

Who Gets the Organs?

By law, the sickest patients nationwide are to have first priority to receive transplants. The local organ procurement organization has the responsibility to recover, preserve, and distribute the organs. That OPO works with the UNOS database to match donor organs to transplant recipients. Livers, hearts, and lungs are the most fragile organs. They are allocated first to patients waiting at the local transplant centers.

Organ transplants can enable seriously ill people to live full, active lives, such as snowboarder Chris Klug, who won an Olympic medal.

If no match is found, the organs are offered to transplant centers in the same UNOS region, then nationally. There is not enough time to fly a heart across the country. But livers and kidneys can go from Seattle to New York in time. A near-perfect match for a kidney (called a six-antigen match) has priority nationwide. It will be flown wherever it is needed.

There have been some controversies about allowing organs to be distributed first within an OPO's region. Some procurement organizations distribute organs over a very large geographic area. An organ could possibly travel many miles to be distributed within the OPO's particular boundary. But the sickest person on the list might be just a few miles away over the border in another OPO's region. In order to assure fairness, in 1998 the government attempted to step in and direct UNOS to have the OPOs choose recipients from a single national list of patients awaiting transplants. After much debate, in 1999 revisions were issued that emphasized the role of the transplant community in policy development. No single national list was necessary. But equal treatment of patients was required regardless of place of residence, celebrity, or socioeconomic status. The government revised its rules. UNOS made some adjustments in sharing procedures. The debate between the government (which controls the funding) and the transplant community (which distributes the organs) is bound to need future adjustments. There is no doubt that the industry will continue its amazing growth and the resources will remain scarce.

There are further controversies about distribution policies. Although it is not proven, some people believe that giving the scarce organs to the sickest patients is wasteful. A desperately ill person might have a smaller chance of doing well with a transplant than a physically stronger patient in an earlier stage of illness. Unfortunately, it is not always possible to tell which persons will do best. At the moment, people who are returning for a second transplant are weighted equally with those who are receiving their first transplant. Is it fair that someone should be provided with a second opportunity when others will die awaiting their first? There is a discussion around which patients should even be listed. Is it fair to list an alcoholic who is still drinking for a new liver? How about a chronic smoker for a lung? How long should they be clean and sober or off cigarettes before they can be listed? Should people who have a history of abusing their bodies be allowed the scarce organs?

There is no doubt that money partly governs access to organ transplant waiting lists in the United States. Some people are denied transplants because they are unable to pay for the transplant or the life-time supply of drugs they would require. In addition, there appear to be racial inequities in the field of transplantation. For example, African Americans are four times as likely as whites to have end-stage renal disease. However, they are less likely to be evaluated and placed on a waiting list for a kidney in a timely manner. They are also more likely to have rare blood types. According to 1999 UNOS data, minorities represent more than half of the persons on the kidney waiting list. They represent fewer than 25 percent of the donations. In 1991, the National Minority Organ and Tissue Transplant Education Program was formed to educate minority communities about transplantation. The program intends to increase minority donation. The hope is also to decrease the number and rate of minorities needing organ and tissue transplants by encouraging healthier lifestyles and behavioral patterns. Finally, there are questions about age limit. Is it fair to keep organs from the elderly? The ages of transplant patients and donors have increased over the years because of medical advances. But the elderly have higher surgical risk factors. Transplantation puts additional stress on the physical system. How do we distribute our few resources? Should scarce organs go to the young who might have more years of health ahead of them? Currently, we cannot always tell which patients will flourish and which will not. If we could, would we make different choices? If members of the medical community are making those choices, do they always agree?

The Organ Shortage

There are a variety of ideas on how to handle the vast shortage of cadaver organs available for transplant. The Department of Health and Human Services has put the responsibility on OPOs to educate the public. They also provide education for hospital staffs to assure that all possible patients are referred. They offer the option of organ and tissue donation to families of potential donors.

Kidney Transplant Waiting List by Race, 2002

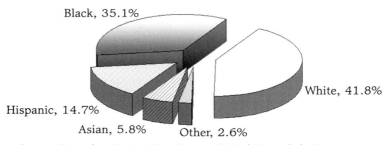

Black, 35.1%
Hispanic, 14.7%
Asian, 5.8%
Other, 2.6%
White, 41.8%

Source: Transplant Patient Data Source, *United Network for Organ Sharing Online*, June 30, 2002, <http://www.unos.org/Newsroom/critdata_wait.htm> (July 25, 2002).

Two other controversial solutions have been debated. The first is to adopt the rule of "presumed consent," which is used in some European countries. The second is paying for organs. If the United States would change the "required request" law to "presumed consent," then organs could automatically be removed from a brain-dead patient unless he or she had previously indicated an objection. Opponents of this idea feel that it would take away the aura of generosity that has been significant in organ transplantation. The idea of donating a "gift of life" to another person can make the tragedy of a loved one's death more meaningful. To require donation may feel more like coercion in the United States, where people value individual freedoms.[2] In the United States, we are careful about infringing upon the rights of individuals. Today, even when a person expresses the desire to donate on a driver's license, the organ procurement organization still has a responsibility to get confirmation from relatives. Signatures are needed on documents that assure consent from the next of kin. The living relatives are given the responsibility for the final choice. Recently, the Health and Human Services released a national donor card. Some hope that this will give transplant officials an ability to proceed with a donation when a family is reluctant.

The great need to procure organs for transplantation has caused the medical community to change their thoughts and ideas about what is acceptable. Most live donors are related to the recipients. Remember Ronald Herrick? In 1954 doctors asked,

"Should we allow him to go through an unnecessary operation to give his twin a kidney?" That question is now a matter of personal choice for people who are related.

The use of anonymous organ donations has raised ethical questions. Until recently, transplant centers turned away people who wanted to donate to a complete stranger. But the University of Minnesota established a program for anonymous kidney donation in 1999. It led to seven transplants by the end of 2000. Doctors at many of the country's leading transplant centers are debating the idea of welcoming "Good Samaritan" donors.[3] A new program called "Hope Through Sharing" was introduced in New England. It allows a noncompatible donor who is related to a person awaiting transplant to donate to a matched person on the top of the cadaver waiting list. This allows their relative to move to the same position on the list.

Organ Selling

Some have suggested that financial benefits that might encourage people to donate should be a normal part of a free-enterprise system. They claim that discounts in health insurance for a potential donor, or a modest payment to help cover funeral services for families, would be a natural incentive to increase donations.[4] However, the 1984 United States National Transplant Act makes selling organs against the law. Organ brokerage is accepted in some countries. This happens especially where poverty makes people desperate for money. Organs have sold for as much as $100,000 in Japan and as little as $1,500 in India.[5]

Some citizens feel that it is the American way to let people do whatever they want with their bodies. They believe that people should be free to sell their own organs in order to raise funds. Some argue that the wealthy have always been willing to let disadvantaged people do other life-threatening things. We let them work in coal mines, they argue. Why not let them sell their organs? The risk is small. After all, they only need one kidney to live.

Opponents say that trading in human body parts is wrong. Commentator Ellen Goodman believes that there are limits to what is tolerable in society. "We have never accepted the notion that the have-nots should become the source of spare parts for the haves," says Goodman. She argues that it is a fundamental abuse of people so desperate that they would have to sell a kidney or half their sight.[6]

In organ transplantation the stakes are high. What is being sold is in severe demand. What is being bought makes a difference between life and death. These facts alone cause some to do whatever they can to procure an organ. In 1999, a kidney was offered for sale on eBay, an auction site on the Internet. The price went up to $5.7 million before the company was alerted and stopped the auction. EBay officials did not know if the auction or bid was legitimate or not. The potential seller and bidders were referred to the FBI. Buying or selling organs in the United States is a felony punishable by imprisonment, a $50,000 fine, or both.[7] There have been reports over the years of people traveling to different countries to buy organs. China, for instance, was supposed to have sold organs from prisoners who had been executed. Between 1988 and 1995, the unethical and illegal taking of organs without parental consent from the bodies of dead children was reported in England.[8] These might be urban legends or true stories. But whenever a commodity is scarce, the potential for greed and the abuse of power is great.

Brain Death Issues

For centuries, the traditional way to define death was by determining the absence of circulation (blood flow), the absence of respiration (breathing), and unresponsiveness (indicating the absence of any neurological activity). The vast majority of people are pronounced dead using these criteria. These people are usually not eligible to be organ donors. For instance, when people are declared dead at the scene of an accident, too much time passes before they can be transported to a hospital for organ removal. By then, their fragile organs are beyond use. As soon as respiration and circulation stop, the body begins to shut down and organs lose their blood supply.

However, medical support systems can now artificially sustain body functions through the use of machines. They can keep a patient breathing and keep the blood flowing through the body. This can happen even when the patient's brain has no possible

When seven-year-old Nicholas Green was killed in Italy, his parents donated his organs to seven people in that country who were waiting for transplants. This bell tower in Bodega Bay, California, was built in memory of Nicholas from dozens of bells, most of them donated by Italians.

hope of revival. For that reason, a new criterion for defining death was declared. The advent of organ transplantation and the need for viable and intact organs was a factor in this decision. After a lengthy debate, in 1981, the President's Commission recommended that a person may be defined as dead on the basis of the irreversible cessation of all function of the brain, including the brain stem (the "whole brain"). Since tissues begin to deteriorate immediately after circulation stops, declaring a patient brain dead allows hospital staff to decide as soon as possible when a person is dying. They can maintain that person on machines after death to prepare them for possible organ donation.

Doctors treating their patients are bound by a code of ethics to do all possible to heal them and to save them from harm. It is important to note that the doctor who pronounces a person dead cannot legally be the same physician who removes organs for transplant. Hospital staff members are committed to the care and recovery of patients. It can be emotionally draining for nurses and physicians in intensive care units to be required to care for people who are dead in order to maintain them for transplantation.[9]

Fear and Confusion

Brain death is a relatively new concept. People may confuse it with being in a coma or a deep state of unconsciousness. Doctors know the difference between a person in a coma and a person who is dead. A comatose person is still very much alive and has neurological activity in the brain.[10]

Change can be very difficult and scary. Advances in technology continue to bring up questions that were not necessary to address in the past. Some people are confused and fearful about brain death. On a questionnaire about donating organs, the primary answer for the reluctance to donate organs was because people were afraid that someone would take their organs before they really died. Some worried that doctors might hasten their death if they needed organs. For some potential living donors there is a deep fear that the organ recovery itself is disrespectful to the body and might kill the donor.[11] There is also a question whether or not the need to remove organs so quickly places families under undue pressure to donate. Some fear that it does not give enough time to grieve before making important decisions.

Religious Issues

Questions about organ transplantation often come from ideas people have about life, death, and what it is to be human. These ideas have roots in religious traditions. Religions have different ideas about issues such as the nature of death and the quality of life. But most of the world's religions either support organ transplantation overwhelmingly or say that it is an individual's personal decision. They would recognize that the gift of an organ is an act of neighborly love and charity. If it came from a live donor, it would need to be freely given and not cause great risk. A few religions, like Shintoism and Buddhism, have strict guidelines about the mutilation of dead bodies. These have caused cultural attitudes in countries like Japan to accept the legalization of organ transplants more cautiously.[12]

The beliefs of religious people around the world are complex and often very different. Most religions acknowledge that healing is a good thing. Most religions believe that accomplishing transplantation by the exploitation of others or by the financial gain of some at the expense of others is improper. Some disagree on the use of fertilized cells for research even if they agree on the need for medical science to find cures for disease.

It is important that people are valued as whole human beings and not simply as a sum of their body parts. Despite the high profile of organ transplantation, fewer than 25,000 organs are transplanted each year in the United States, which has a population of 270 million. Most practicing physicians encounter only a few transplant recipients during their practice. Some say that the government should take some of the $120 million it spends on organ transplantation and invest it into programs that prevent disease, such as immunizations. Others point to the amazing advances that have been made in organ transplantation in the past few years alone.

Medical advances are in the news daily. Actor Michael J. Fox contributes to research on Parkinson's disease in hope that the disease that is causing his central nervous system to degenerate can soon be cured. Christopher Reeve is a famous actor who had an accident while riding his horse. He invests in research that he hopes will someday lead to the repair of his damaged spinal cord and allow him to walk again. Are these even possible hopes and dreams for the future? The significant technological and surgical advances in medicine that have contributed to the continuing success of organ transplantation and the understanding of the immune system point to a resounding yes.

Chapter Notes

Chapter 1. Russell's Story

1. Mary Lane Gallagher, "Sehome Grieves for Lost Students," *The Bellingham* (Washington) *Herald*, March 30, 1999, p. A1.

2. Personal interview with Susan Schofield, October 10, 2000.

3. "Critical Data: U.S. Facts About Transplantation," *United Network for Organ Sharing Online*, July 19, 2002, <http://www.unos.org/Newsroom/critdata_main.htm> (July 25, 2002).

4. "Facts of Life," *National Transplant Society Page*, n.d., <http://www.organdonor.org/facts.cfm> (August 10, 2000).

5. *Questions and Answers About Organ Donation* (Mercer Island, Wash.: LifeCenter Northwest Donor Network, May 24, 2000).

6. Letter to Susan Schofield from Scott Ward, Organ Recovery Coordinator, LifeCenter Northwest Donor Network, April 12, 1999.

7. Schofield interview.

Chapter 2. A History

1. Alexis Carrel, "Nobel Lecture, December 12, 1912," *Nobel e-Museum Page,* n.d., <http://www.nobel.se/medicine/laureates/1912/press.html> (July 3, 2001).

2. Lee Gutkind, *Many Sleepless Nights: The World of Organ Transplantation* (Pittsburgh: University of Pittsburgh Press, 1990), p. 25.

112

3. Scott McCartney, *Defying the Gods: Inside the New Frontiers of Organ Transplants* (New York: Macmillan Publishing Company, 1994), pp. 52–53.

4. "Hall of Fame/inventor profile: Willem J. Kolff," *National Inventors' Hall of Fame Page*, n.d., <www.invent.org/hall_of_fame/88.html> (July 3, 2001).

5. Joseph E. Murray, "Nobel Prize Lecture: The First Successful Transplants in Man," *Kidney Transplantation: Past, Present, and Future Page*, n.d., <http://www.stanford.edu/dept/HPS/transplant/html/murray.html> (August 1, 2001).

6. Thomas E. Starzl, *The Puzzle People, Memoirs of a Transplant Surgeon* (Pittsburgh: University of Pittsburgh Press, 1992), p. 87.

7. McCartney, p. 53.

8. Starzl, pp. 88–89.

9. "Jean Dausset—Biography," *Nobel e-Museum Page*, n.d., <www.nobel.se/medicine/laureates/1980/dausset-bio.html> (July 5, 2001).

10. McCartney, p. 54.

11. Frank Stuart, Michael M. Abecassis, and Dixon B. Kaufman, *Organ Transplantation* (Georgetown, Tex.: Landes Bioscience, 2000), pp. 546, 550.

12. Jeffrey Prottas, *The Most Useful Gift* (San Francisco: Jossey-Bass Publishers, 1994), p. 6.

13. McCartney, p. 57.

14. Rene J. Duquesnoy, "Early History of Transplantation Immunology (Part 2 of 2)," *University of Pittsburgh Medical Center Page*, n.d., <http://tpis.upmc.edu/tpis/immuno/wwwHistpart2.html> (July 11, 2001).

15. "First Successful Kidney Transplant Performed, 1954," *People and Discoveries: A Science Odyssey Page*, 1998, <http://www.pbs.org/wgbh/aso/databank/entries/dm54ki.html> (July 7, 2001).

16. Starzl, p. 277.

17. Gutkind, pp. 39–40.

18. Starzl, p. 289.

19. Stuart, Abecassis, and Kaufman, p. 50.

20. Ibid., p. 45.

21. Starzl, p. 114.

22. Paula T. Trzepacz and Andrea F. DiMartini, eds., *The Transplant Patient* (Cambridge, England: Cambridge University Press, 2000), pp. 9–10.

23. McCartney, pp. 239–240.

24. Trzepacz and DiMartini, p. 10.

25. Ibid., p. 16.

Chapter 3. Precious Organs

1. "Dialysis," *National Kidney Foundation Page*, May 15, 2001, <http://www.kidney.org/general/atoz/content/dialysisinfo.html> (August 2, 2001).

2. Personal interview with Steve and Marla Morrow, July 13, 2001.

3. Frank Stuart, Michael M. Abecassis, Dixon B. Kaufman, *Organ Transplantation* (Georgetown, Tex.: Landes Bioscience, 2000), p. 105.

4. Ibid., p. 177.

5. Mark Porter, "Strength of the Heart," *The Bellingham* (Washington) *Herald*, March 22, 2001, p. A1.

6. Stuart, Abecassis, and Kaufman, p. 269.

7. "A Patient's Guide to Liver Transplant Surgery: About Your Liver," *University of Southern California Liver Transplant Program Page*, n.d., <www.livertransplant.org/pateintguide/whattheliverdoes.html> (August 1, 2001).

8. McCartney, p. 44.

9. "Press Conference Promotes Organ Donation, Celebrates First Successful Living Donor Liver Transplant," *The University of Chicago Hospitals and Health System Page*, November 1999, <www.uchospitals.edu/news/LLD10.html> (May 7, 2001).

••

10. "Donors," *United Network for Organ Sharing Online*, 2001, <http://www.unos.org/Newsroom/critdata_donors.htm> (July 25, 2002).

11. Stuart, Abecassis, and Kaufman, p. 259.

12. "Facts About Lung Transplantation," *Cystic Fibrosis Foundation Page*, n.d., <http://www.cff.org/publications09.htm> (June 14, 2001).

13. "Data Highlights: Intestinal Characteristics, 2000 Annual Report of the Organ Procurement and Transplantation Network," *United Network for Organ Sharing Online*, <www.unos.org/Data/anrpt00/ar00_datahigh_11.htm> (July 5, 2001).

14. Paula T. Trzepacz and Andrea F. DiMartini, eds., *The Transplant Patient* (Cambridge, England: Cambridge University Press, 2000), p. 275.

15. "Bone Marrow with Organ Transplants Reduces Rejection of Transplanted Organ," *Doctor's Guide: Global Edition, 2000*, <www.pslgroup.com/dg/f880a.htm> (August 10, 2000).

Chapter 4. The Immune System

1. S. Gard, "Presentation speech, Nobel prize in Physiology or Medicine, 1960," *Nobel e-Museum Page*, <www.nobel.se/medicine/laureates/1960/press.html> (July 8, 2001).

2. Nancy J. Nordenson, "Blood Typing and Crossmatching," *aHealthyMe! Page*, n.d., <http://www.ahealthyme.com/article/gale/100084944> (July 21, 2001).

3. Robert Finn, *Organ Transplants: Making the Most of Your Gift of Life* (Sebastopol, Calif.: O'Reilly, 2000), p. 270.

4. Ibid., p. 48.

5. Ibid., p. 117.

6. H.F. Pizer, *Organ Transplants: A Patient's Guide* (Cambridge, Mass.: Harvard University Press, 1991), p. 23.

7. Jeffrey Prottas, *The Most Useful Gift* (San Francisco: Jossey-Bass Publishers, 1994), p. xvii.

8. "Bone Marrow With Organ Transplants Reduces Rejection of Transplanted Organs," *Doctor's Guide: Global Edition Page*, 1995, <http://www.pslgroup.com/dg/f880a.htm> (July 22, 2001).

Chapter 5. The Business of Organ Transplants

1. Robert Finn, *Organ Transplants: Making the Most of Your Gift of Life* (Sebastopol, Calif.: O'Reilly, 2000), p. 3.

2. Jeffrey Prottas, *The Most Useful Gift* (San Francisco: Jossey-Bass Publishers, 1994), p. 1.

3. Ibid., p. 19.

4. "Critical Data: U.S. Facts About Transplantation," *United Network for Organ Sharing Online*, July 19, 2002, <http://www.unos.org/Newsroom/critdata_main.htm> (July 25, 2002).

5. Ibid.; "Waiting List," *United Network for Organ Sharing Online*, 2002, <http://www.unos.org/Newsroom/critdata_wait.htm> (July 25, 2002).

6. Scott McCartney, *Defying the Gods: Inside the New Frontiers of Organ Transplants* (New York: Macmillan Publishing Company, 1994), p. 120.

7. Prottas, p. 42.

8. Ibid., p. 51.

9. Phillip G. Williams, *Life From Death: The Organ and Tissue Donation and Transplantation Source Book with Forms* (Oak Park, Ill.: The P. Gaines Co., 1989), pp. 9–10.

10. Prottas, pp. 16–17.

11. *Background*, educational leaflet (Mercer Island, Wash.: LifeCenter Northwest Donor Network, May 25, 2000).

12. Paula T. Trzepacz and Andrea F. DiMartini, eds., *The Transplant Patient* (Cambridge, England: Cambridge University Press, 2000), p. 21.

13. Finn, p. 33.

14. Prottas, p. 159.

Chapter 6. The Future of Organ Transplants

1. Richard Merritt, "Anti-Oxidant Enhances Islet Cells' Ability to Produce Insulin in Experimental Models," *Duke University News Service Page*, April 8, 1997, <http://www.dukenews.duke.edu/Research/islet.htm> (July 18, 2001).

2. "Beta Cell Transplants," *The Diabetes Mall Page*, 1997, <http://www.diabetesnet.com/betacl.html> (July 18, 2001).

3. Robert Finn, *Organ Transplants: Making the Most of Your Gift of Life* (Sebastopol, Calif.: O'Reilly, 2000), p. 272.

4. "Discouraging Results in Fetal Nerve Cell Transplants," *Thinkquest: News*, March 19, 2001, <http://library.thinkquest.org/28000/news.php3?all=yes> (July 26, 2001).

5. "Novel Approaches to Graft Protection," *Novartis: Transplantation and Immunology Page*, <http://www.transplantsquare.com/health/druginfo/newdev/graft/graft.htm#top> (July 26, 2001).

6. Paula T. Trzepacz and Andrea F. DiMartini, eds., *The Transplant Patient* (Cambridge, England: Cambridge University Press, 2000), pp. 292–293.

7. Michael D. Lemonick, "Brave New Pharmacy," *Time*, January 15, 2001, p. 66.

8. Guy Gugliotta, "Artificial Heart Put into Human," *The Seattle Times*, July 4, 2001, p. A1.

9. Michael D. Lemonick, "Reviving Artificial Hearts," *Time*, May 8, 2000, p. 65.

10. Finn, p. 277.

11. "Artificial Eyes, Turbine Hearts," *Businessweek Online*, March 20, 2000, <http://www.businessweek.com/2000/00_12/b3673025.htm?scriptFramed> (September 9, 2000).

12. Gunjan Sinha, "Organ Cowboy," *Popular Science*, October 1999, p. 68.

13. "A Pioneer in Surgery," *The James Hardy Archives, The University of Mississippi Medical Center Page*, n.d., <http://www.umc.edu/hardy> (July 8, 2001).

14. Rebecca D. Williams, "Organ Transplants from Animals: Examining the Possibilities," *U.S. Food and Drug Administration Page*, n.d., <http://www.fda.gov/fdac/features/596_xeno.html> (July 26, 2001).

15. "Frequently Asked Questions about Xenotransplants," *TransWeb.org: All About Transplantation and Donation Page*, <www.transweb.org/qa/qa_txp/faq_xeno.html> (March 28, 2001).

16. Williams.

17. Ibid.

18. "The Promise of Tissue Engineering," editorial, *Scientific American*, April 1999, <http://www.sciam.com/0499issue/0499ezzell.html> (July 26, 2001).

19. David J. Mooney and Antonios G. Mikos, "The Promise of Tissue Engineering," *Scientific American*, April 1999, <http://www.sciam.com/April1999/0499issue/0499mooney.html> (July 26, 2001).

20. Ibid.

21. Ibid.

22. Paul Recer, "Questions, Answers About Stem Cells," *MEDLINEplus*, July 4, 2001, <http://www.nlm.nih.gov/medlineplus/news/fullstory_2564.html> (July 28, 2001).

23. Jessica Reaves, "The Great Debate Over Stem Cell Research," *TIME.com*, July 11, 2001, <http://www.time.com/time/nation/article/0,8599,167245,00.html> (July 25, 2001).

24. Laura Meckler, "Panel Rejects Permanent Cloning Ban," *Yahoo! News*, July 11, 2002, <http://story.news.yahoo.com/news?tmpl=story&cid=514&ncid=716&e=3&u=/ap/2002071> (July 22, 2002).

Chapter 7. The Ethics of Organ Transplants

1. Jeffrey Prottas, *The Most Useful Gift* (San Francisco: Jossey-Bass Publishers, 1994), p. 153.

2. Ibid., p. 77.

3. Benedict Carey, "Giving of Themselves," *LA Times: Calendarlive*, October 2, 2000, <http://www.calendarlive.com/top/1,1419,L-LATimes-Search-X!ArticleDetail-5933,00.html> (July 28, 2001).

4. Stuart J. Youngner, Renée C. Fox, and Laurence J. O'Connell, eds., *Organ Transplantation: Meanings and Realities* (Madison, Wis.: University of Wisconsin Press, 1996), p. 102.

5. Lee Gutkind, Many *Sleepless Nights: The World of Organ Transplantation* (Pittsburgh: The University of Pittsburgh Press, 1990), p. 83.

6. Gary E. McCuen and Therese Boucher, *Terminating Life: Conflicting Values in Care* (Hudson, Wis.: Gary E. McCuen Publications, Inc., 1985), p. 138.

7. Phillip G. Williams, "Appendix B: Revised Uniform Anatomical Gift Act," *Life From Death: The Organ and Tissue Donation and Transplantation Source Book with Forms* (Oak Park, Ill.: The P. Gaines Co., 1989), p. 213.

8. Associated Press, "Report Details Organ Raids at U.K. Hospital," *The Bellingham* (Washington) *Herald*, January 31, 2001, p. A9.

9. Youngner, Fox, O'Connell, p. 45.

10. "Coma," *Neurology Channel Page*, n.d., <http://www.neurologychannel.com/coma/> (July 30, 2001).

11. Gutkind, p. 96.

12. John Lewis, "Japan Legalizes Organ Transplants," *CNN Interactive Page*, October 16, 1997, <http://www.cnn.com/WORLD/9710/16/japan.transplants/> (August 10, 2000).

Glossary

allograft—Living tissue or an organ placed into another person who is not genetically identical.

anastomosis—A surgical technique for sewing together the ends of blood vessels or intestines.

antibody—a substance released by the body's cells that will destroy, weaken, or neutralize the invading matter.

antigens—Molecules on the surface of the body's cells that carry the genetic code and trigger an immune response in an organ transplant recipient.

autograft—Living tissue taken from one part of a person's body and transferred to another location in the same body.

bone marrow—Spongy tissue found in the bones that contains blood cells and platelets.

brain death—The irreversible cessation of function in the entire brain, including the brain stem.

cadaver—The body of a dead person.

chimerism—The peaceful coexistence of both donor and recipient cells without rejection following a transplant.

donor—One who gives one or more organs to be transplanted.

graft—Material such as living tissue or an organ surgically placed into a body to replace similar tissue or organs.

immune system—The body's system of defense against foreign invaders.

immunosuppressants—Antirejection drugs that are given to a recipient in order to keep his or her immune system from destroying the donor organ.

ischemic time—The time period that an organ can be cooled and stored apart from its blood supply before it is safely transplanted.

islet cells—Clusters of cells from the pancreas that secrete insulin.

isograft—Living tissue or an organ placed into the same person or one genetically identical.

leukocytes—White blood cells that set up an attack on substances that are foreign to the body.

pathogen—An agent that causes diseases.

recipient—The person who receives new organs to replace the organs that are failing.

rejection—The failure of a recipient's body to accept transplanted tissue or organ because it is incompatible with the immune system.

renal—Related to the kidneys.

xenotransplantation—The transplantation of an organ or tissue from one species into another.

For More Information

American Diabetes Association
Attn: Customer Service
1701 North Beauregard Street
Alexandria, VA 22311
1-800-DIABETES (1-800-342-2383)

American Heart Association
National Center
7272 Greenville Avenue
Dallas, TX 75231

American Liver Foundation
75 Maiden Lane, Suite 603
New York, NY 10038
1-800-GOLIVER (1-800-465-4837)

National Kidney Foundation
30 East 33rd St., Suite 1100
New York, NY 10016
800-622-9010
212-889-2210

National MOTTEP
(Minority Organ Tissue Transplant Education
Program)
2041 Georgia Avenue, NW
Ambulatory Care Center, Suite 3100

Washington, D.C. 20060
202-865-4888
800-393-2839

National Transplant Society
853 Sanders Road, Suite 314
Northbrook, IL 60062
847-283-9333

United Network for Organ Sharing (UNOS)
1100 Boulders Parkway, Suite 500
PO Box 13770
Richmond, VA 23225-89770

Further Reading

Durrett, Deanna. *Organ Transplants*. San Diego: Lucent Books, Inc., 1993.

Kittredge, Mary. *Organ Transplants*. Philadelphia: Chelsea House Publishers, 2000.

Murphy, Wendy. *Spare Parts: From Peg Legs to Gene Splices*. Brookfield, Conn.: Twenty-First Century Books, 2001.

Winters, Adam. *Organ Transplant: The Debate Over Who, How, and Why?* New York: Rosen Publishing Co., 2000.

Yount, Lisa. *Issues in Biomedical Ethics*. San Diego: Lucent Books, 1998.

Internet Addresses

Gift of Life: Donor Program
<http://www.donors1.org/>

United Network for Organ Sharing (UNOS)
<http://www.unos.org/>

TransWeb: All About Transplantation and Donation
<http://www.transweb.org/>

Index

A
AIDS, 73
allograft, 22
anastomosis, 19
animal organs, transplanting, 33, 90–93
antibodies, 26, 57, 58, 86
antigens, 26, 57, 62
artificial organs, 86, 88–90
    artificial heart, 88–89
    artificial kidney, 89
artificial kidney machine, 23, 38
autograft, 22

B
Baby Fae, 33, 90
Barnard, Christiaan, 29
B cells, 57
blood typing, 61–62
body parts, transplanting, 32, 55
bone marrow, 54–55, 68, 84
Borel, Jean-Francois, 29
bowel transplants, 32
brain death, 31, 63, 107–110
Burnet, Frank Macfarlane, 60

C
cadaver donors, 11, 12, 21, 55, 71, 72, 103
Carrel, Alexis, 19, 21, 23
children and transplants, 46, 52, 54

chimerism, 33–35, 84
Clark, Barney, 88
cloning organs, 55, 93–96
consent, 72, 75, 104
Cooper, Joel, 32
cornea transplants, 54
cross matching, 62
cyclosporine, 29–30, 61

D
Dausset, Jean, 26
dialysis, 23, 38–39
drug cocktails, 27–28

E
ethical issues, 17, 97–111

F
Food and Drug Administration (FDA), 32

G
genetic engineering, 84, 93–96
Gibbon, John H., 28
Gohlke, Mary, 29
Goodman, Ellen, 106
grafts, skin, 22, 55, 58

H
Hamburger, Jean, 26
Hardy, James D., 28, 90
heart transplants, 28, 29, 45–47, 89
Herrick, Richard, 23–24
Herrick, Ronald, 23–24, 104
human leukocyte antigens (HLA), 26, 62–63